SATAN'S KINGDOM

Bristol and the *Transatlantic* *Slave Trade*

PIP JONES

past & present
press

Published by Past & Present Press
92 Sefton Park Road, St Andrews, Bristol, BS7 9AL

enquiries@pastandpresentpress.co.uk
www.pastandpresentpress.co.uk

Satan's Kingdom: Bristol and the Transatlantic Slave Trade
ISBN 978 – 0- 9532082 –1-0

First published 2007 by Past & Present Press
Copyright Pip Jones. All rights reserved.

Past & Present Press welcomes manuscripts for consideration for
publication. Do, not, however, send irreplaceable material. All
material is submitted entirely at the sender's risk.

The publication of *Satan's Kingdom, Bristol and the Transatlantic
Slave Trade* has been supported by Abolition 200

Design and layout: Gillian Marles

(Methodist New Rooms)

John Wesley made one of his periodical visits to the city in March 1788, and preached on the 6th upon the burning question of the slave trade. His sermon was interrupted by what he deemed to be a supernatural occurrence:

*"A vehement noise arose, and shot like lightning through the whole congregation. The terror and confusion was inexpressible. The benches were broken in pieces, and nine-tenths of the congregation appeared to be struck with the same panic. In about six minutes the storm ceased. None can account for it without supposing some preternatural influence. **Satan fought lest his kingdom should be delivered up.**"*

ONE

The earliest documented information about Bristol's involvement in a trade in slaves comes from the time of the Norman Conquest. Wulfstan, Bishop of Worcester since 1062, came to Bristol to preach a series of searing sermons against the practice of selling slaves. Bristol was so notorious for this practice that the town was known throughout the country as 'The Step Mother of all England'.[1] Men, women and children were bought, often from their families, or kidnapped from the surrounding countryside and further afield. They were sold to the Ostmen (descendants of Norse raiders) who lived in southern and eastern Ireland. English youths were most favoured as personal servants as they were believed to be 'more reliable' than native slaves and less likely to run away as they had little chance of escaping and returning home. Young women were often first made pregnant as this increased their value.[2]

Wulfstan's preaching raised awareness of the sin of trading in people and for a time the trade declined and virtually died out. However, within a few decades it had re-emerged and is recorded as flourishing during the troubled reign of King Stephen. The civil war that his reign produced made it easier to acquire prisoners of war and to make successful kidnapping raids.

In 1135 Stephen of Blois had seized the throne on the death of his uncle, King Henry I. The true claimant to the throne was Henry's only surviving child, his daughter, Mathilda, married to Geoffrey Plantagenet, Count of Anjou. From 1139, on her arrival in England, until 1148 Mathilda led her followers in a civil war against Stephen, which continued when she eventually returned to France, her forces being led by her eldest son, Henry Plantagenet. In 1153, however, Stephen was compelled to acknowledge Henry as his heir and the following year on Stephen's death, Henry II became king. His strength, enthusiasm and authority did much to reduce the lawlessness that had made slaving so easy.[3]

Of course, a form of slavery existed in England apart from the process that captured, purchased or kidnapped people for sale. The social ranks in Anglo-Saxon and Norman England started with the king, and then proceeded down to the lower classes, who existed in a state of near-slavery. Below the ranks of the nobility came the geneat or 'sokeman', freemen and land owners in their own right, craftsmen and merchants, who might choose to give their allegiance to a Lord. Under them in the social hierarchy were the cotsetlas, literally 'cottagers', villeins working the land or following a craft. They were, however, essentially free men who worked their own land, even if they owed service and had to offer some fixed labour to their Lord.

In the lowest social group were the geburs or serfs; these people were tied to land they did not own or have any legal rights to, working at trades whose profit went to their Lord. In theory, every chattel they possessed belonged to the Lord. A serf could not marry, bequeath property, leave his job or his village without permission, and owed a large variety of services to his Lord. The children of serfs were also counted in that class; the only way for a serf to become free was either to purchase freedom, to be granted it by their Lord, or to run away and avoid capture for a year and a day. However, even a serf could not be bought and sold like a slave.

Some people actually chose to become serfs. If an individual or a family experienced poverty and starvation, they might offer their services as serfs to a Lord. In return for being tied to his land and service, they would receive protection, work, somewhere to live and food to eat.

Below the serfs were slaves. The Domesday Book actually listed 9% of the people as being slaves, that is, some 25,000 individuals. As the decades passed after the Norman Conquest, the ranks of slaves decreased; the Lords found it was easier to pay a small wage to a man than to own him and have to support him and his family indefinitely. The advent and broader use of coins also made the payment of wages easier and more cost effective.[4]

Serfdom in general really began to decline in the 14th century with the terrible outbreak of the Black Death in England. It has been estimated that about 30% of the working population died. This meant that there was an enormous demand for labour, which the serfs were only too ready to exploit. Larger towns and cities were crying out for workers and the serfs could hide from anyone trying to take them back to their 'owners'. Some Lords set about trying to force their resentful and rebellious people to stay; others offered better conditions and fewer obligations to persuade them. By the 16th century, the days of serfdom were coming to an end. In 1577 William Harrison wrote:

> 'As for slaves and bondmen, we have none; nay such is the privilege of our country by the special grace of God and the bounty of our princes, that if any come hither from other realms, as soon as they set foot on land they become so free of condition as their masters, whereby all note of servile bondage is utterly removed from them.'[5]

One peculiar attempt to revive the state of serfdom was recorded in Bristol in the spring of 1586. Lord Stafford of the manor of Thornbury claimed that the brothers, Richard and Thomas Cole, were 'villeins appurtenant', that is that they were his serfs and that he had every right to seize them and their property as his own. Richard Cole was then Mayor of Bristol and chief magistrate, a wealthy merchant related to several prominent local families by marriage (his wife was Alice, sister of John Carr, founder of Queen Elizabeth's Hospital). The Coles approached the Privy Council who ordered Stafford to stop harassing them until the case could be heard in court, although it seemed that there was no case to answer – the Cole family had been freemen as long as anyone could remember. Stafford, however, was obsessed with what he saw as his rights. He abandoned the idea of a court case, which he would certainly have lost, and tried to violently kidnap the Coles instead. In May 1587 the Privy Council again ordered him to stop threatening the brothers. When he failed to do so yet again, he was ordered to appear before the Queen's Council in London in December. The Corporation records hold no more information on the case, so presumably the Council had sufficient authority to stop Stafford taking any further action and Richard and Thomas Cole avoided enslavement.6

Stafford may have got the idea from a similar escapade in the 1470s, recorded in Bristol's Great Red Book, when Lord de la Warre tried to do the same thing to an elderly, wealthy merchant, William Bird, ex-Mayor and Sheriff of Bristol, on the grounds that he was a runaway serf. Lord de la Warre insisted he had the right to seize the person of the merchant, as well as all his immediate family and take his property. Fortunately the rest of the Bristol Corporation took Bird's side and were able to prove that although his grandfather had lived on a de la Warre manor, his ancestors were freemen from Birmingham.7

—

The trade in African slaves by British merchants had its origins in the division of the world in 1493 by Pope Alexander. With the discovery of the New World by Christopher Columbus in 1492 on behalf of Spain, the kings of Spain and Portugal argued about the ownership of the new lands, both actual and yet to be discovered. To solve their differences, Pope Alexander passed the Bull *Inter Ceatera*. This assigned all lands to the west of the Atlantic to Spain or Portugal, on a line dawn 270 leagues west of the Cape Verde Islands. Everything to the west of the line belonged to Spain, everything to the east, to Portugal.

This division might have passed relatively quietly, had not gold and silver been discovered. At this point, the rest of Europe protested at Spain's annexation of these lands. Francis I of France told the Spanish ambassador, 'I have never seen a clause in the last will of Adam conceding such exclusive control to Kings Manoel and Charles'. Spain and Portugal, however, maintained their right, under threat of arms, to these new, rich lands.8

England also made a major discovery when in 1497 John Cabot set foot in Newfoundland. Several years later, his son Sebastian got as far as Hudson's Bay. However, their main product being fish, these newly-discovered lands failed to inspire much fervour9.

By 1570 Spaniards had colonised the Indies and South America; they settled in Mexico, Peru and the Caribbean, enslaving the local populations to work on the estates – labour the Spanish colonists considered beneath them with their new-found status as land-owners. The native peoples died in their thousands. In 1576 an epidemic carried off an estimated 40-50% of the Indians in Mexico;10 in the Caribbean, the Carib and Arawak people almost completely disappeared. The Caribbean Islands in particular had small populations and as the people died, there were too few left to keep the population levels high enough to provide slave labour in sufficient quantities. As the only resource of the Islands was crop farming, the need for labour was acute.[11]

To supply unskilled labour, the Portuguese offered a solution – they had influence in West Africa where local chieftains sold their prisoners of war as slaves to Arab traders, as they had done for centuries. Why should these people all go to the Middle East; why should not some go to the West Indies and South America? The Portuguese bought Africans on the Guinea Coast and shipped them to Hispaniola in the Indies, where they traded them for sugar and hides. From Hispaniola the slaves could be sent to anywhere in the Spanish American Empire or to Portuguese-controlled Brazil.

Africans were easier to enslave than local native Americans. The Indians were settled on the land of their ancestors, they knew who and what they were and had a history of family and kinship. They already had a political and social framework in place and were unwilling to adopt foreign practices. Indians in any area usually spoke a common language; they could escape, receive help and hide amongst their own kind. They knew how to grow local produce and were less easily taught to grow new crops. Furthermore, when sickness killed many of their numbers, their birth rate did not rise to meet the shortfall – once these people were gone, there was no one to replace them.

In contrast, the Africans were in a foreign country thousands of miles from their homes. They had no ties to the new land and no links with the indigenous people. They could be selected so that they came from different tribes and did not even speak a common language. They would be less likely to try to escape as they had nowhere to go. Because of all this, they could more easily be taught European ways and the husbandry of new crops. Moreover, if they died, new slaves could always be bought.[12]

The Portuguese solution was greeted enthusiastically by Fr. Las Casas, a Catholic monk who had travelled to South America to redeem souls. He saw this as an alternative to the enslavement of his new flock of native converts. He wrote to the Spanish Emperor Charles V to allow 12 Negroes to be imported for every Spanish settler. Charles agreed and assigned the lucrative trade to a court favourite, Lorenzo de Gomenot, who sold the contract to a firm of Genoese merchants. For 25,000 ducats, this syndicate had the right to import 5,000 Negroes into Spanish territories each year.

In a very little time, Fr. Las Casas realised what he had done and desperately tried to halt the vile trade he had encouraged, but it was too late.[13] He wrote of his feelings, relating to the treatment of native Indians and Africans, in his book, *Historia de las Indias*, published in 1550, insisting that, 'the enslavement of the Negroes was as unjust as that of the Indians.'

The Portuguese had a lengthy history of African trade. They had been among the first European nations to trade with Africa during the reign of Prince Henry the Navigator, Duke of Viseu (1394-1460), son of King John I and Queen Philippa (daughter of John of Gaunt, son of Edward III of England). Prince Henry had first concentrated on trade with the Canaries and Azores (earning himself the title of Lord of the Isles). Still he desired to discover new lands to rule (he was a younger son) and 'heathen' peoples to convert. He had heard stories about Prester John, the mythical king of a Christian nation in Africa and he set out to find him, as well as the fabled southern route to India and the East that by-passed the Muslim middle-men. His ships never reached the Cape of Good Hope (this would happen in 1488), but they did get as far as the Gambia River and made contact with the city of Timbuktu.[14]

By 1400 the Portuguese merchants were primarily concerned with trading for African gold. King John II (1455-1495) extended Portuguese influence in Africa and it was he who authorised the buying of slaves, although the traders were still principally interested in gold and ivory. They bought a few slaves, who went to Europe as domestic servants or were traded to other African tribes for more gold. In both Spain and Portugal there were still small numbers of slaves kept, mostly Africans and Arabs. They were never a major source of labour, however, as slaves were expensive and peasant labour was plentiful and cheap.

The primary area of trade for Portugal was in Mauritania, Senegambia and the Gold Coast; they set up trading posts on Arguin Island (off Mauritania), the Cape Verde Islands (off Senegambia) and the Guinea Gulf Islands, Sao Tomé and Principé (off Guinea).[15]

By the mid-1400s the Portuguese were trading about 800 slaves each year; this rose steadily to 1,500-2,000 by the 1480s. Some time around the turn of the century, they established trade connections with the previously unexploited Kingdom of Kongo. Here they were able to barter for more gold and for slaves. The number exported each year now rose to 2,600.[16]

At first, slaves were taken to the Portuguese controlled islands – the Azores, Madeira, the Cape Verde Islands, Sao Tomé, and the Spanish Canaries. On these islands, sugar was already in production, the labour being supplied by the Islanders, Spanish Moors and then African slaves. By the 1450s, Madeira sugar was on sale in London and 5-600 slaves were being shipped to the Islands each year. The decline of sugar production on the Islands by the mid-1500s was paralleled by the rise of production in the West Indies. Demand in Brazil, the Caribbean and South America opened new markets for such slaves as the Portuguese were able to buy.[17]

In these early years, the trade in slaves was still relatively small, given the exorbitant Spanish import duties – these taxes were so rigidly enforced that there was a shortage of slaves in the mid-1500s.

This, of course, left an opening for any enterprising merchant. In 1562 John Hawkins of Plymouth sailed to the Guinea Coast 'which place by the people of the country is called Tagarin', filled up with 300 slaves and headed to the West Indies. According to the Portuguese, Hawkins raided their settlement and stole the slaves; according to him, he bought them and agreed to the Portuguese telling their story to avoid trouble with the Spanish. He even put on a fake show of strength, he said, in order to support their story.

In Hispaniola, according to Hawkins, the same thing happened; he made a show of force, supposedly making the local Spanish estate owners buy his slaves – the Spanish later reported that Hawkins had attacked and robbed their town and had been forced to leave behind a number of slaves. He used the money to buy pearls, gold, ginger, sugar and hides, returning to England with a handsome profit. His voyage was described by Richard Hakluyt in his book, *The Principal Navigations*, published in 1589. For many years to come, Hawkins and other British adventurers would trade with the Spanish in the same illegal manner.[18]

Hawkins was not the first Englishman to trade with the Portuguese in Africa. The Bristol Captain Thomas Wyndham of Marshfield Park, Somerset, had sailed with three ships from Kingroad in 1552 to the Barbary Coast, to break into the Portuguese markets in Africa. His ship carried 'good quantity of linen and woollen cloth, coral, amber, jet and diverse other things well accept by the Moores'. He, however, had not been interested in African slaves; in fact, British merchants at this time were opposed to becoming involved in slavery, preferring to trade in gold, wood and ivory.[19] The Guinea Merchants, as they were called, wrote that the trade in humans was contrary to the laws of God and Man. It was not until the foundation of the Royal Africa Company during the early Stuart period that slaves were added to the list of generally traded commodities.

Notes
1   Brown, HG & Harris, PJ, Bristol England (1967), p.14.
2   Robinson, Derek, *A Shocking History of Bristol* (1973), p.11.
3   Brown, H.G. & Harris P.J., op cit, p.14-5.
4   Brooke, Christopher, *From Alfred to Henry III 871-1272* (1961), p.42.
5   Walvin, James, *Slavery and the Slave Trade* (1983), p.20
6   Latimer, John, *Sixteenth-Century Bristol* (1908), p.85-6
7   Latimer John, *Sixteenth-Century Bristol* (1908), p.30-1
8   Thomson, George Malcolm, *Sir Francis Drake* (1973), p.11-3
9   Brown, H.G., Harris, P.J., *Bristol England* (1967), p.57-9
10   Thomson, George Malcom, *Sir Francis Drake* (1973), p.16
11   Dresser, Madge & Giles, Sue, *Bristol And Transatlantic Slavery* (1999), p.43
12   Klein, Herbert S, *The Atlantic Slave Trade* (1999), p.20
13   Everett, Susanne, *History of Slavery* (1997), p.31-2
14   Stanford, Peter, 'The Cape Horn Road, Part IV: Portugal Opens the Ocean Doorway to Wider World', Sea History, 77 (Spring 1996), 14-17
15   Klein, Herbert, *The Atlantic Slave Trade* (1999), p.9-10
16   Klein, Herbert, op cit, p.10-11
17   ibid p.13-4
18   Thomson, George Malcom, op cit, p.17-21
19   MacInnes, CM, 'Bristol and the Slave Trade', McGrath, Patrick (ed), *Bristol in the 18th Century* (1972), p.162

TWO

With English interest in Canada established and blossoming trade links in the Caribbean, Englishmen now looked to establish their own bases in the Americas. Sir Walter Raleigh founded England's first colony in North America in 1584. In honour of Queen Elizabeth, he named it Virginia. From his new lands came tobacco and potatoes, Raleigh's famous contributions to English culture. The story of his servant, believing his master to be on fire, throwing a bucket of water over him when he sat smoking, is a well-known part of Tudor history. The Dutch were possibly the first to trade slaves with this new colony; 1619 saw one of the first recorded cargoes of Negro slaves being landed in Virginia.[1] At this point only a few English, French and Dutch ships were in competition with the limited number of Portuguese traders.

After Raleigh, the settlement of North America occurred in a piecemeal fashion. Settlements grew into provinces, which would become states. Not unsurprisingly, given Bristol's maritime and mercantile roots, several of these fledgling provinces were founded by Bristolians, or those with a Bristol connection. Both Massachusetts and Rhode Island had counties of Bristol; Rhode Island also had a town called Bristol.[2]

Sir Ferdinando Gorges (1566-1647), a West Country merchant whose family lived at Wraxall just outside Bristol, founded a Virginia Company to trade with America in 1606. James I authorised him and his backers, who included Lord Chief Justice Popham, to found two colonies, with a charter that a local historian, Bancroft, called 'the first colonial charter under which the English were planted in America'. In 1607 two ships loaded with potential settlers left Plymouth for a settlement called St George in what they called Northern Virginia, actually a part of New England, only to return a year later when the colony failed.[3]

Nothing daunted, Gorges approached James I again in 1620 and was rewarded with a patent giving him and his supporters (some of whom were Bristol merchants) control over the whole of North America, from the Atlantic to the Pacific. They alone had the right to trade between England and America, and the sole rights to fishing off the East Coast. Gorges' Virginia Company was prepared to lease trade and fishing rights to other organisations such as the Bristol Merchant Venturers, under the supervision of the New England Council. They also suggested that anyone who subscribed £12 10s would be eligible for a 'gift' of 200 acres of land in America. To encourage settlement in their new lands, if a family emigrated, they would receive an additional 100 acres for each family member, at a nominal rent of 5s per annum. People in Bristol and Somerset were actively encouraged by the Crown to take up this offer and settle the colonies.

At the age of 70 Sir Ferdinando received a Royal Charter from Charles I in 1639 whereby he and his heirs were given the province of Maine in New England. In return, the Crown reserved the right to 20% of all gold and silver mined and all pearls fished and an annual rent of a quarter of wheat.[4] Sir Ferdinando Gorges became known as the Father of English Colonisation in North America and his interest in the colonies was demonstrated in his book, *Briefe Narration of the Originall Undertakings of the Advancement of Plantations into the Parts of America.* He spent most of his life in Plymouth and died in England. He is buried in St Budiana church, St Budeaux, Plymouth, Devon.[5]

In 1624 a group from Dorset set out to colonise Massachusetts, founded by the Rector of Holy Trinity church, Dorchester. John White (1575-1648), the Patriarch of Dorchester, never went to America himself, but he founded not only the colony, but also the Massachusetts Company in 1626. Sir Richard Saltonstall principally funded this venture; John Endicott was the first governor and White sent out two ministers for his flock in May 1629, Francis Higginson and Samuel Skelton.[6]

Admiral Sir William Penn of Bristol served both Commonwealth and King, sailing with the force that took Jamaica in 1655. He died in September 1670 and was buried in St Mary Redcliffe church, next to his mother. King Charles II repaid a loan to the Admiral by granting a charter to his son, William Penn (1644-1718) to found a colony in America. Thus Pennsylvania was conceived, and as Penn was a non-conformist and a Quaker, it was to be administered as a Quaker settlement. Penn also founded the town of Philadelphia (literally, the place of philo-delphus – 'Love of the Brother'). Unfortunately his attitudes to religion and the British government frequently got him into trouble with British officials, including a spell in prison. He wrote *No Cross, No Crown*, an affirmation of rule by the people, without church or state intervention.[7]

When setting up his colony, Penn applied to his friends and colleagues in Bristol. They founded the Free Society of Traders in Pennsylvania, and Penn granted them 20,000 acres of land for a settlement. Nicholas Moore, a Bristol lawyer, led the local contingent to America, and Penn brought out a similar group from London. In 1696 he again visited Bristol and married, as his second wife, Hannah Callowhill, a local heiress. Their children inherited Penn's American property on his death.[8]

Throughout the 17th century, the number of colonies and the size of their populations steadily increased. However, until 1700 the number of slaves coming into North America was relatively small. Unlike the Spanish in South America, the British immigrants expected to work their own land, aided by a few slaves – bond-servants from England, some native Americans and a very few Africans.

In the 17th century, the American centres for the reception of slaves coming into the colonies were in the Chesapeake Bay area (including Virginia, Maryland and North Carolina), and South Carolina and Georgia.[9]

Thanks to its lack of natural resources and the abundance of suitable ports, New England eventually became the centre for slave trading; most of those slaves imported into the southern states came through New England from the Caribbean. Massachusetts, particularly Salem and Boston, were the most prominent slaving ports until 1750; meanwhile Providence, Newport and Bristol, in Rhode Island, were also centres. To begin with, the governors of Rhode Island were against enslaving anyone, black or white, but this gradually gave way, until by the 1750s Rhode Island was pre-eminent in the trade in Africans.[10]

In the early 1700s New England ships sailed to Africa and bought slaves, only to trade them in the West Indies for goods, particularly sugar, for home consumption. They operated a Triangular Trade in reverse, as Lorenzo Johnston Green noted in his book, The Negro in Colonial New England 1620-1776:

> 'From New England's many ports, trim, sturdy ships, built from her own forests, carried to the West Indies much needed food and other commodities, such as surplus beans, peas, hay, corn, staves, lumber, low-grade fish, horses, dairy produce, and a miscellaneous assortment of goods. When the captains of these vessels were able to exchange their cargoes for rum, they would next proceed directly to Africa. There they bartered their rum for slaves who they transported to the West Indies where they disposed of them for rum, sugar, molasses and other tropical products or for bills of exchange.'[11]

The sugar and molasses were carried to New England, distilled into rum, and along with trinkets, bar iron, beads and light-coloured cloth, taken to Africa and exchanged for Negroes.

The goods listed on a bill of lading for an American ship differed quite considerably from a British one. The emphasis was on home-produced merchandise, and the quantities of rum reflected Rhode Island's large distilling industry. The Lading Bill of the Sierra Leone, sailing from Newport, Rhode Island, to Africa in 1754 reads:

> '54 Hogsheads, 10 terces, 8 barrels and 6 half-barrels Rum, 1 barrel sugar, 60 musketts, 6 half-barrels powder, 1 box beads, 3 boxes snuff, 1 barrel tallow, 2 barrels beef, pork and mutton, 22 lbs bread, 1 barrel mackerall, 6 shirts, 5 jacketts, 1 piece blue Callico, 1 piece Chex, 1 mill, Shackles and handcuffs...'[12]

The southern colonies concentrated on cash crops. For example in South Carolina, rice and indigo were the main crops in the late 17th century, and tobacco was the principal crop in Virginia. The farms were relatively small; the owners supplemented their workforce with a few servants and slaves but once the farms grew into plantations the demand for more labour and therefore for slaves, grew with them.

The purchase of these people tended to be made in the West Indies. The earliest slave ship recorded was the Desire, built in Marblehead, Massachusetts Bay, in 1636. She sailed from Salem to the West Indies; here she traded New England goods and a few enslaved Pequot Indians for African slaves. In 1671 Sir John Yeamans of Bristol and the West Indies brought slaves into South Carolina from Barbados to work on his newly acquired plantation.

When early American merchants went to Africa, they brought back only a few slaves, usually to fill any space left after taking their usual cargo on board. It was not until 1654 that the *Rainbow* was recorded as going from America to Africa specifically to trade for slaves.[13]

Numbers of slaves in the American colonies were initially very small – in 1625 there were records of only 23 slaves. In 1706 South Carolina recorded the importing of only 24 slaves in a year; two years later, Governor Nathaniel Johnson wrote that there were about 4,000 settlers in South Carolina and about the same number of slaves in total. In 1708, for example, Virginia was estimated to have a total of 12,000 slaves. By contrast, in 1726 in South Carolina, there were an estimated 40,000 slaves, with an annual arrival of 1,000 new people. As the number of slaves grew, the laws passed to keep them helpless and subservient grew in severity. Not only did the owners fear the growing numbers of slaves, they feared the influence of the Spanish in Mexico and southern North America who might encourage the Negroes to revolt in order to further their own desire for conquest from the south. To justify their position, the slave-owners stigmatised the Africans as an inferior race, fit only for servitude.[14]

The owning of slaves was universal in all the provinces from the earliest times of settlement, although some states, like Ohio, Indiana and Illinois, soon passed bills to outlaw slave trading in their territories. When the people of Virginia migrated north west, they arrived in states that had abolished slave trading but when they moved into the unsettled lands that would become the provinces of Tennessee, Kentucky, Mississippi, Alabama, Louisiana and Missouri, they brought the acceptance of slavery with them.

The people of Virginia, a province with a large number of Bristolian settlers, owed the success of their agricultural endeavours to the fertility of the land, the long growing season, the high rainfall and the abundance of river transport and good coastal harbours. The state as a whole was both for and against slavery. East of the Blue Ridge Mountain, in the area known as The Tidewater and The Piedmont, were the plantations, run by slave labour; west of the Ridge were the mountains and the Shenendoah Valley, where there was a preponderance of smaller farms, run with few or no slaves. Many of the smaller farmers came from the Quaker, anti-slavery state of Pennsylvania, but slavery stayed on the statute books as the wealth and power stayed in the hands of the plantation owners.[15]

Virginia was an early and prolific producer of tobacco, although in the mid-18th century there was a move towards food production, particularly wheat. There was a problem in that the southern plantations tended to put their money in land and slaves, while the northern grain producers, like Pennsylvania and New York, put their investments into machinery, particularly mills to grind the wheat into flour.

Like sugar, tobacco required a large, fairly skilled workforce. The seedlings were

Bristol Trade cards for tobacco, 18th century. In England, 'Virginian' became synonymous with top quality tobacco products. (Bristol's Museums, Galleries & Archives)

grown separately and replanted into the 'hills' in the fields. Here they had to be watched and constantly pruned, to encourage growth only in the broad lower leaves. They were then harvested, cured and packed. This latter task was highly skilled, as the leaves had to be packed in such a way as not to tear or bruise the leaf. Virginia prided itself on producing the finest quality leaf, so it was a matter of national pride to ensure that all tobacco coming out of the province should be the very best. In England, 'Virginian' became synonymous with top quality tobacco products.

Not only did slaves grow, harvest and pack the tobacco, but slaves also made the staves for the barrels known as hogsheads; they made the hoops and nails to complete the barrels, they drove the wagons and sailed the barges that delivered the barrels to the dockside warehouses. Slaves loaded and unloaded the ships, and provided some of the crew – by law, no crew could contain more than 33% slaves (in case of mutiny or absconding), and no slave could be a ship's captain.[16]

—

British colonies in the West Indies were founded in the early 1600s. Columbus had discovered the islands on his first voyage, landing on the Bahamas and visiting Cuba and Hispaniola. On his second voyage, he landed on Dominica, Puerto Rico, Hispaniola and Jamaica, but the Spanish had mostly ignored these islands, so much so that native tribes still lived there. British, French and Dutch smugglers and pirates used them as bases of operations and it required these groups to be driven out before a mixture of settlers from all three countries could start working the land in earnest. It was not unusual to find more than one nationality on the same island – St. Kitts, for example, first settled in 1625, had both English and French settlers. Sir Thomas Warner had led the English party that settled St. Kitts.

English and Dutch settled Barbados. The Dutch has first established their colonies in Portuguese Brazil, before they moved into the Caribbean. At first they supplied the French and English with materials, produce and slaves, then in the 1650s they founded their own colonies on Barbados, Guadeloupe and Martinique. Ten years earlier the Dutch, along with the French and the English, had settled in the Lesser Antilles, producing tobacco and indigo, and then sugar.

In 1640 there were 52,000 English on Barbados, Nevis and St Kitts. Five years later, the government of Barbados reported that the population comprised 18,300 white males and 5,680 slaves. Of the white population, 60% were landowners; the average holding was 10 acres and the principal crop, tobacco. By 1680 there were 38,000 slaves recorded (almost all African by birth), and 350 sugar plantations. Some 175 planters now owned more than half the land; the average size of a plantation was 220 acres and was worked by an average of 100 slaves. The annual importation of slaves was 1,300 and by 1700 there were estimated to be 50,000 slaves on Barbados.[17]

In 1645 Sir George Downing, Cromwellian and Carolinian political secret agent and developer of Downing Street, wrote to his cousin, John Winthrop, in Massachusetts:

> *'If you go to Barbados, you shall see a flourishing Island, many able men. I believe they have bought this year no less than a thousand Negroes, and the more they buy, the better able they are to buy, for in a year and a half, they will earn (with God's blessing) as much as they cost...'*[18]

In 1655 a force was sent under the command of General Venables and Admiral Penn to take Hispaniola from the Spanish. When their attack failed, they turned their invasion force on the less well defended Jamaica, which they were able to take quite easily.[19] By the early 1700s, it was the foremost sugar-producing British-owned island. The number of slaves grew rapidly – 74,000 in 1720, to 173,000 in 1760. By contrast, the English population stood at 10,000. At this point, Jamaica was home to almost half the total number of slaves in the West Indies. About 95% of the slaves were working in the rural sector, and 75% were engaged in producing sugar.[20]

The farmers on the Islands began to grow cotton and tobacco, which required little capital and relatively light labour. By the 1650s, however, the crop range had increased to include ginger, indigo – and sugar. This latter crop was labour intensive, and the need arose for slaves – Africans for field labour and English to perform the skilled jobs (e.g. mason, smith, clerk). Irish slaves (prisoners of war) were seen as least desirable; they were reputed to be lazy and politically inclined to side with England's enemies. An English prisoner of war seized during Monmouth's Rebellion who did very well in the colonies was Azariah Pinney, who came as an indentured prisoner, and rose from factor (or agent) to estate owner and merchant.

The growing of sugar required a large number of African labouring slaves. The cane had to be planted in a trench and left to grow for 14-18 months. It was then cut, crushed in a mill to extract the liquid sugar that was then boiled and allowed to set. The crystal or 'muscavado' sugar was separated out from the liquid molasses, which could be distilled into rum. The old cane sent out shoots called 'ratoons' which could be cut and planted to provide a second, poorer crop; eventually, however, the canes would have to be grubbed up and a new trench planted.[21]

By the late 17th century, English colonies in North America and the West Indies were established and growing. One of their chief needs was for a labour force. The native people were unused to hard field work, and were susceptible to European diseases introduced into the colonies; they died of over-work, cruelty, sickness and melancholy. On the once well-populated mainland, the native peoples had been radically reduced by the time that the English and French colonised the West Indies, so they had to rely at first on bond-slaves and indentured servants from their own countries. However, as the 17th century drew to a close, the European labour requirement was growing and indentured servants who would once have chosen emigration to find work were now staying at home, with the offer of higher wages. It therefore became essential to their survival that the colonists find a reliable supply of workers and, again, Bristol, amongst others, was able to oblige.

The decline in the number of people prepared to choose to be indentured servants was occasionally balanced by the appearance of prisoners of war who were given the option of becoming bond-slaves or dying on the scaffold. The merchants and plantation owners of Bristol were not slow to take advantage of the situation, as and when it arose. In August 1648 the army of Oliver Cromwell was victorious over the Scots army in Lancashire and the prisoners of war were made available as slaves to be transported to the colonies as an alternative to execution. The Commons Journal of the Bristol Corporation of the 4th September indicates that 'the gentlemen of Bristol applied to have liberty to transport 500 of the prisoners to the plantations', which permission was readily granted. The Battle of Worcester in 1651, followed by battles at Chester, Stafford and Ludlow, provided yet more prisoners, and again Bristol merchants were to the fore in acquiring them for transportation.[22]

In July 1652 the Mayor of Waterford was requested to send Irish rebels from prison to Bristol, where they could be shipped to the West Indies. The merchants Robert Cann, Robert Yate and Thomas Speed signed the request, and later Thomas Speed was to request a further 200 men to ship to Barbados.[23]

The supply of prisoners of war, however, was unreliable. Once peace was established, a new source of supply had to be found. Ordinary prisoners guilty of capital crimes were offered the alternative of transportation to execution but even then the number of eligible prisoners was not large enough to keep up with the demand from the growing colonies. Transportation would eventually become a recognised sentence for some crimes, the length of the period to be spent in servitude abroad to be decided by the seriousness of the crime.

There were, however, still not enough suitable people being sent to the colonies and it seems that unscrupulous merchants resorted to enticing or even kidnapping young people; they would be shipped out and sold as if they were prisoners. In September 1654, the Corporation passed an ordinance that all 'boys, maids and others' who were transported as servants to the colonies had to have their indentures of service entered in the Tolzey Book. This was to try and prevent young people being taken against their will – there was a fine of £20 on any ship's captain who allowed anyone on board who had not had their indentures registered.[24]

The ordinance, of course, had little effect – the need, and the rewards, were too great. Firstly, the Corporation found it difficult to inspect all ships just before they sailed; if they had time, kidnapped servants could be smuggled on board as the ship was leaving. Fully-armed crews were difficult to confront by single officials. There was also the difficulty that those who administered the laws were the very merchants who were shipping the kidnapped youths out, or who relied on cheap colonial labour for their trade. In September 1655 two men were found guilty of 'man stealing' and sentenced to an hour in the pillory with a placard listing their crimes around their necks. Normally, the crowd, when they discovered what they had done, would have

Settlement in the West Indies, with plantations owned and run by Bristol families, provided a good deal of the cities wealth in the 18th century. Map of the West Indian Islands (Bristol's Museums, Galleries & Archives)

seriously injured or killed the men, but the merchants, many of whom were justices, ordered a guard to protect them.[25]

The disgrace of this slavery came to a head in 1685, with Monmouth's Rebellion and the arrival in Bristol of Judge Jeffreys. It had been established by royal agreement that rebels should be transported – the Judge had written to James II from Taunton that some 850 West Country rebels had been sentenced to transportation. They were worth about £10-15 each, and he recommended that the Queen, her ladies in waiting and the King's favourites should each receive the profits on the sale of a number of these men.

On 21 September, Judge Jeffreys came to Bristol, and went to the Guildhall to set up a court, ostensibly to try the captured rebels. He began the proceedings by insulting the Bristol gentlemen assembled to act as jury, calling them rebels, saying they were hen-pecked and that they were involved in the crime of kidnapping ('I hear the trade of kidnapping is of much request. They [the justices] can discharge a felon or traitor, provided they will go to Mr. Alderman's plantation at the West Indies.').

There were few cases for Jeffreys to hear (six men were sentenced to death of whom three were reprieved) and he turned his attentions to the Mayor and Aldermen. He had been told that his first assumption had been right, that it was common practice of the servants of the Aldermen to approach prisoners and tell them that they were to be hanged; the only way to save themselves was to request transportation. Jeffreys also heard that the Aldermen operated a ring to make sure that each took his turn to receive prisoners on his own plantations and even those who did not actually take part connived with those that did and turned a blind eye.

Judge Jeffreys severely reprimanded the Aldermen. He began with Sir William Hayman, the Mayor, saying, 'Sir, Mr. Mayor, yes I mean, kidnapper! And that old justice on the bench [Alderman Lawford], an old knave; he goes to the tavern, and for a pint of ale he will bind people servants to the Indies. A kidnapping knave! I will have his ears off before I go forth of town.'

A series of charges were now read, including one that the Mayor had benefited from the transportation of a pickpocket. Jeffreys harangued him, 'You are worse than the pickpocket who stands at the bar. I hope you are a man of worth, I will make you pay sufficiently for it!' He then fined the Mayor £1,000, 'for suffering a boy committed to Bridewell to go beyond the seas' and forced him to enter the dock and plead like a common criminal – Hayman pleaded not guilty to the charges. He was then taken in custody, whilst Jeffreys gave his opinion that he would like to order Hayman hanged, had he not respected the city so much.

The charges were then made against Sir Robert Cann, Alderman Lawford, William Swymmer, John Napper and Robert Kirk; each was ordered to pay £5,000 in sureties to answer the charges at the next King's Bench. Jeffreys wrote to Lord Sunderland immediately afterwards, telling him in detail what had transpired and warning him to tell the King not to listen to anyone asking for pardons for these men before he, Jeffreys, had had a chance to talk to the king himself. In the event, the merchants

Judge Jeffreys visited Bristol in September 1685. He was quick to criticise the city councillors,
calling them rebels, saying they were hen-pecked, and that they were involved in the crime of
kidnapping. 'I hear the trade of kidnapping is of much request. They [the justices] can discharge
a felon or traitor, provided they will go to Mr. Alderman's plantation at the West Indies.'
Portrait of Judge Jeffreys by William Claret, 1680. (National Portrait Gallery)

were able to keep the charges in abeyance for 3 years, by which time James II was no longer king, and all charges were dropped under a general amnesty from William III and Mary II.[26]

Trading in slaves was practised almost worldwide and Englishmen might fall victim as well. In October 1674 John Knight, a cooper, petitioned the Bristol Court for help in ransoming his brother, a Bristol sailor. He had been seized, along with his ship, by Turkish pirates and sold as a slave. The ransom was set at £130, which Knight did not have – he asked the Court's assistance in raising the money. The Court itself could not help, but he was given permission to appeal to the citizens of Bristol, specifically the churchwardens of Bristol churches were instructed to make his case known to their congregations and request subscriptions towards the appeal. Knight's was not an isolated case – seamen of all nations ran a risk of being kidnapped and sold into slavery.[27]

In the mid-1600s Bristol was the second city in England, and the second port. Naturally, Bristol merchants were soon involved in the profitable trade in goods from the West Indies – and African slaves.

Although few Bristolians actually colonised the West Indies, a lot went to America. Between 1654 and 1685, some 10,000 Bristolians emigrated to North America and became prominent in tobacco production, particularly in Virginia.[28] The work force, however, was almost entirely white at this point – prisoners, rebels and bond servants. Back in England, only a few black servants appear in Bristol records before the 18th century.

One of the earliest references comes from the records of a dispute heard by the Court of Star Chamber in 1579. Amongst the papers is a reference to Sir John Young who was one of those under investigation. Around 1560 it was said that he 'did appointe a blacke moore to keep possession of his garden' at his 'great house', a high status house (with a Red Lodge) that stood on the site of the Colston Hall.[29] Some time later came the next references to Africans, like Joan Smyth and Peter, both 'blackamores' (who died in 1603 and 1610 respectively[30]), Cattalena from Almondsbury who died in 1625[31], Solomon, dying in 1631, who belonged to William Hayman, and Marye, servant to William Edmonds, baptised in 1632.[32]

Cattelena is remembered by the record of the probate inventory of her goods after her death in May 1625. She is described as a 'Single Woman (a Negro)', and her goods comprised:

> *a cow, value £3 10s; a bed and bedding, 10s; 2 pewter pots, candlesticks, tin bottle & a dozen spoons, 5s; 3 earthen dishes & 24 trenchers, 8d; a table cloth, 6d; wearing apparel, £2; a coffer and 2 boxes, 3s 4d.*

There are also two early examples of African slaves accepting Christianity. At this time it seems that this acceptance earned them some protection. In 1640 there was a record of a woman called Frances, described as a 'blackamoor maid', 'which thing is somewhat rare in our days and nation, to have an Ethiopian or Blackamoor to be…truly converted to the Lord Jesus Christ, as she was.' There is no mention of her situation; the writer seems more interested in the fact that, 'this poor Ethiopian's soul sorrowed much for God, and she walked very humble and blameless in her conversation to her end.' When she died:

> '…*this Aetheopian yielded up ye spirit to Jesus that redeemed her, and was honourably interred, being carried by ye Elders and ye chiefest of note of ye Brethren in ye Congregation…to ye grave…by this we may see that Scripture made good, that is, "God is no respecter of faces, but among all nations…".'* [33]

The second lady was Dinah Black; her case is recorded in the Minutes of the Court of Aldermen in July 1667. She was the 'servant' of Dorothy Smith, had been baptised and was an enthusiastic member of her local congregation. Ms Smith, however, sold her and she was forced on board a ship to take her to 'the plantations'. Somehow her well-wishers were able to find her and have her released. The Corporation Minutes state that she should be allowed to remain free and to earn her living until the next Quarter Sessions when her case would be heard in full and resolved. Although it is not stated, Latimer took it to mean that Dinah was an African slave.[34]

In the same year that the 'blackamore' Solomon died, 1631, Charles I issued a monopoly in the Guinea trade to a group of London merchants, and two years later, added a monopoly in the trade with Canada. This latter move particularly annoyed Bristol merchants as it was one of their number, John Cabot, who had first sailed to Newfoundland. Trade with Africa had belonged to a group of London merchants since the Tudor period, when the monarch would assign rights of trade in one specific area to an organisation or individual who would pay fees to the Crown and use their own resources to build up that trade.

London merchants, receiving more royal attention, tended to be the recipients of such monopolies, to the resentment of the merchants of cities such as Bristol. It is even possible that London's monopolies and the ill-feeling they engendered were partly to blame for Bristol merchants siding with the Parliamentary cause against the Crown.

With the restoration of the monarchy, 1660 saw the formation of the Africa Company in London, dedicated to trade in gold and ivory with Africa. This replaced any previous affiliations of merchants and set African trade on a regular footing, allowing for greater exploitation. In 1663 a second charter was issued to the Company of Royal Adventurers of England Trading to Africa, under the patronage of the Duke of York. The guinea coin was struck in commemoration. This time, specifically, the charter mentioned various items of trade, including slaves. The Secretary of the Company wrote to Francis Lord Willoughby, Governor in Chief of the Caribbean Islands:

'My Lord, the Royal Company being very sensible how necessary it is that the English Plantation in America should have a competent and a constant supply of Negro-servants for their own use of Planting, and that at a moderate Rate, have already sent abroad, and shall within eight days dispatch so many Ships for the Coast of Africa as shall by God's permission furnish the said Plantations with at least 3,000 Negroes, and will proceed from time to time to provide them a constant and sufficient succession of them so as the Planter shall have no just cause of complain of any Want.' [35]

Bristol and her merchants immediately complained about the restrictive practices of this monopoly. A petition was presented to Parliament from Bristol merchants and plantation owners like Ferdinando Gorges of Bristol and Barbados. They insisted that the success of the colonies depended on a good supply of slaves; they went on to suggest that the Africa Company sold their best Negroes to the Spanish, whilst selling the remainder to British colonists at inflated prices, thanks to their closed market. They went on to point out that ships trading with Africa and the Colonies brought out a lot of British goods and that they would return with sugar, indigo, ginger, tobacco and many other things for processing and sale in Britain. This meant a great stimulus for British manufacturing, which would be reduced or even lost if a rigid monopoly was in force. In 1689 a complaint was submitted on behalf of the Barbados planters:

'There never want fair Pretences for the foulest Monopolies. But what do they pretend for this. They will tell you that (to the common Good and Benefit of the English nation) they can deal with the People of Africa to much better advantage, by being a Company. And so they might, if they could shut out other Nations. But since the Dutch, French, Danes, Swedes, and others trade thither... they can shut out none but the poor English... And it plainly appears that 'tis not upon the People of Africa, but upon the English Planters in America, that they make their advantage...

'Of all the Things we have occasion for, Negroes are the most necessary, and the most valuable. And therefore to have them under a Company, and under a Monopoly, where by their prices are more than doubled, nay almost trebled, cannot but be most grievous to us. Many an Estate hath been sunk and many a Family hath been ruined, by the high prices they give for Negroes...' [36]

In 1673 the King issued a new patent to the recently formed Royal Africa Company, succeeding the now-defunct Africa Company whose rights the new Company had bought out.

A year later, a royal proclamation was issued in Bristol ordering merchants to stop infringing on the rights of the Company; they were forbidden to trade in either goods or slaves between the African coast and the Americas.[37] The Merchant Venturers, already well established, quietly ignored this order; if anything, Bristol's Africa trade grew during these years of prohibition. In fact, several Bristol merchants, like Edward Colston and Nathaniel Pinney, actually joined the Royal Africa Company.

In 1689, with the accession of William & Mary, all previous monopolies were overruled, and the question of Africa trade was opened again. In the same year, an Act was passed limiting the monopoly of the Africa Company but they still controlled the forts along the African coast and could therefore, to a certain extent, control the approaches to the coastal trade by others.

The Bristol merchants had no intention of letting the lucrative Africa trade remain a monopoly of London. In November 1695 John Cary, a Bristol merchant, published *An Essay on the State of England in relation to its Trade, its Poor, and its Taxes, for carrying on the present War against France.* He set out the city's objections to London-based monopolies, both the Royal Africa and the East India Companies. He wrote on the subject of slavery that it was:

> '…a trade of the most advantage to this kingdom of any we drive, and as it were all profit; the first cost being little more than small matters of our own manufacture, for which we have in return gold, [elephant's] teeth, wax and Negroes, the last whereof is much better than the first, being indeed the best traffic the kingdom hath, as it doth occasionally give so vast an employment to our people both by sea and land.' [38]

In 1696 the Royal Africa Company applied to have its monopoly re-established by Parliament; not unsurprisingly, Bristol was opposed to this and lobbied hard. Bristol merchants submitted a report to Parliament maintaining that the 3,000 slaves transported each year by the Company were wholly inadequate for the needs of the colonies. Only by extending the number of traders would there be an increase in the supply. The clothiers and weavers of the city added that their trade was now dependent on supplying goods to use as barter for slaves.[39] Over the next two years, other ports joined Bristol's protest, and even the estate owners in the colonies added their voice, as they needed more and cheaper slaves. A government-inspired 10% tax on African trade goods was also fought, as was the proposal that all merchants should pay towards maintaining the forts. It was argued they were now obsolete as trade centres and useless as defensive sites – what was needed was a regular patrol by Royal Navy frigates, and free trade.

In the end, Parliament denied the Royal Africa Company their bill, but passed one opening the trade with the proviso that those merchants visiting the African coast should contribute towards the maintenance of the forts. They also levied a 10% tax on African goods, reduced to 5% for redwood, and waived for gold, silver and Negroes.[40] In 1708 the Royal Africa Company tried again to win back their monopoly, but again, they were met by opposition from Bristol, and failure; the 10% tax was also repealed.

At the start of the 18th century, the trade with the colonies was described as 'the cream of Bristol's commerce'.[41] The West Indies were seen as being slightly more important than North America, since the latter supplied tobacco and cotton, whilst the former provided both of these along with hardwoods, dyewoods, sugar, molasses and rum. The appearance of good cane sugar coincided with the growth in the consumption of tea from India, each luxury item complementing the other, until these two became necessities rather than luxuries.

Bristol's trade, however, was not exclusively with the New World. There was always contact with Ireland, the Channel Islands and other British ports. Beyond these, Bristol traded with Scandinavia, the Baltic, the Netherlands and Germany, to the city's great advantage. The Irish trade had been a city mainstay for centuries: imports included salt beef and pork, linen and yarn, leather, hides and timber; exports consisted of manufactured goods and, latterly, colonial products. From the Baltic came paper, steel, wine and brandy, timber, linen and other fabrics.[42]

In 1700, of the ships that arrived in Bristol, 79 were from European ports, 68 from Ireland, 55 from the West Indies, 38 from North America, and none direct from Africa.[43]

As far as trade with the West Indies went, the bulk of imports came through the ports of London, Liverpool and Bristol. Goods were received, refined and treated, and sent on throughout Britain and Europe. Bristol companies produced such items as brassware, glass and ceramics, cotton and linen stuffs, spirits, muskets and ammunition – all of which could be used for trade with Africa or exported direct to the colonies for their own use. The ships carrying these goods were engaged on the Triangular Route, from Bristol to the Guinea Coast, then on to North America and the West Indies, and back to Bristol, or the Direct Route, from Bristol to America and the West Indies, and back..

In 1701 a recorded total of 165 ships left the port. In 1709 there were 57 ships specifically engaged on the Triangular Route.[44] The whole of the 18th century was a period of expansion – the population of the city rose from c.20,000 in 1700 to c.64,000 by 1800. Trade with Ireland, Scandinavia, Germany, the Netherlands and the Iberian Peninsula would be out-stripped by that with the West Indies and North America. Bigger and better ships were built and the port grew to accommodate them.

Notes
1   Klein, Herbert S, *The Atlantic Slave Trade* (1999), p.43
2   Latimer, John, *The History of the Society of Merchant Venturers of the City of Bristol* (1903), p.152
3   Latimer, John, *The Annals of Bristol in the Seventeenth Century* (1970), p.27-8
4   Latimer, John, *The Annals of Bristol in the Seventeenth Century* (1970), p.72-4
5   Greenwood, Douglas, *Who's buried where in England* (1982), p.103
6   Greenwood, Douglas, op cit(1982), p.163
7   ibid p.115
8   Latimer, John, *The Annals of Bristol in the Seventeenth Century* (1970), p.475-6
9   Klein, Herbert S, op cit, p.43
10   Duigan, Peter & Clarendon, Clarence, *The United States and the African Slave Trade 1619-1862* (1963), p.5
11   Duigan, Peter & Clarendon, Clarence, op cit, p.6
12   ibid, p.9
13   ibid, p.2-3
14   ibid. p.1-5
15   McColley, Robert, *Slavery and Jeffersonian Virginia* (1964), p.3-9
16   McColley, Robert, op cit, p.18-9
17   Klein, Herbert S, op cit, p.28-30
18   McColley, Robert, *Slavery and Jeffersonian Virginia* (1964), p.13
19   Cordingly, David, *Life among the Pirates, The Romance and the Reality* (1995), p.59
20   Klein, Herbert S, op cit, p.32]
21   Pares, Richard, *A West-India Fortune* (1968), p.15
22   Latimer, John, op cit, p.223
23   ibid p.223
24   ibid p.254-5
25   ibid p.25
26   ibid p.433-7
27   ibid p.368
28   Little, Bryan, *The City and County of Bristol* (1954), p.142
29   Public Record Office, STAC 5/S 14/26
30   Lindegaard, DP, *Bristol Roots: Black Bristolians in the 17th, 18th and 19th Centuries* (1990), p.33, 40
31   Bristol Record Office (BRO), Bristol Probate Inventories, No. 18
32   Lindegaard, DP, op cit, p.40, 28
32   Hayden, R (ed.), *The Church of Christ in Bristol* (1640), p.101
33   Latimer, John, op cit, p.344
34   Plimmer, Charlotte & Denis, Slavery, *The Anglo-American Involvement* (1973), p.19
35   Plimmer, Charlotte & Denis, op cit, p.25
36   Latimer, John, op cit, p.368
37   Latimer, John, *The History of the Society of Merchant Adventurers of the City of Bristol* (1903), p.178
38   Latimer, John, *The Annals of Bristol in the Seventeenth Century* (1970), p.485
39   McInnes, CM, *'Bristol and the Slave Trade'*, McGrath, Patrick, *Bristol in the Eighteenth Century* (1972), p.164-5
40   Little, Bryan, *The City and County of Bristol* (1967), p.158
41   Minchinton, Walter, *'The Port of Bristol in the Eighteenth Century'*, McGrath, Patrick (ed.), *Bristol in the Eighteenth Century* (1972), p.129-30
42   Minchinton, Walter, *'The Port of Bristol in the Eighteenth Century*, McGrath, Patrick (ed.), Bristol in the Eighteenth Century (1972), p.131
43   Latimer, John, *The Annals of Bristol in the Eighteenth Century* (1970), p.6, 89

THREE

As trade with the West Indies and North America increased in the first half of the 18th century, so did the traffic in slaves by Bristol ships and merchants. In 1700, 46 ships were involved in trade with the West Indies; between 1708 and 1712, some 13 ships a year were going specifically to Africa to trade for slaves. In the 1720s this number increased to an average of 25 a year, and between 1728 and 1732, this average rose to 48.

At the beginning of the century about 70 ships were trading with Ireland each year, some of the trade goods being colonial in origin. By comparison with the colonial business, the Irish trade had been, and would continue to be, of great importance to Bristol. The Irish ports also provided a stop for Bristol ships on their way to Africa, the West Indies and America, to take on food, water and, occasionally, linen and yarn (in 1731 the *Union*, Agent, James Laroche & Co., Master, William Williams, sailed from Bristol to Cork, then to Africa, Jamaica and back to Bristol).[1] Despite the lure of the wealth of the West Indies and Africa, it took a year to cover the triangular route (one voyage) whereas in the same period, a ship could manage several trips to Europe or Ireland.

Bristol was already the second port of England after London; now it became the second city in size. It also became the regional centre for the South and West, as well as for South Wales. For a city of such importance, it lacked outward grandeur. The city was still based around the medieval centre of Broad Street, Wine Street, Corn Street and High Street, which met at the site of the High Cross. The streets were narrow, averaging about 20 feet in width, with tall, over-hanging houses. The streets were notoriously dirty, with an open channel running down the centre and paved with rough stone blocks; pigs hunted rubbish in these open drains. The rivers Avon and Frome carried shipping into and out of the city and acted as sewers for the citizens and their livestock.

In 1700 the population stood at about 20,000 – by the end of the century it would rise to some 64,000 and 61,153 in 1801 according to the city's tax records.[2] Throughout this time, the city was physically growing. In the early decades, Queen's Square was laid out and its houses constructed, the Corn Exchange was erected and put into service and St. Thomas's Church was built. The city was expanding beyond its medieval centre and moving out into the suburbs – merchants used their new wealth to build houses in the surrounding countryside. Goods from the city were sent by coaster to Bristol Channel ports and around to London and Gravesend. They went by Severn Trow to Bewdley, Bridgnorth, Frampton, Gloucester, Newnham, Stroud, Tewkesbury, Upton and Worcester; by road on five main routes, north to the Vale of Berkeley, south into Somerset, and east to Tetbury and Oxford, Bath and Warminster, and Chippenham and London. The writer, Daniel Defoe, noted that

Bristol merchants:

> '...maintain carriers just as the London tradesmen do, to all the
> principal countries and towns from Southampton in the south, even to the
> banks of the Trent north and tho' they have no navigable river that way,
> yet they drive a very great trade through all these countries.'[3]

The reputation of the city was that it was driven by trade. Thomas Cox wrote in his *Magna Britannica* in 1727:

> '...the People give themselves to Trade so entirely, that nothing of the
> Politeness and Gaiety of Bath is to be seen here ... all are in a hurry,
> running up and down with cloudy looks and busy faces, loading, carrying
> and unloading goods and merchandises of all sorts from place to place; for
> the Trade of many nations is drawn hither by the Industry and the
> Opulency of the People. This makes them remarkably insolent to
> Strangers, as well as ungrateful to Benefactors, both naturally arising
> from being bred, and become rich by Trade, as (to use their own Phrase)
> to care for no Body, but whom they can gain by...'[4]

We are told, in fact, that, 'the very clergy talk of nothing but trade and how to turn the penny'.[5] The demand for slaves on the farms and plantations in the West Indies and America fuelled trade. Industries grew up in Bristol to provide the goods that would be bartered for slaves in Africa, as well as the materials and goods needed by the plantation owners and workers themselves. This latter meant, in practical terms, clothing for English and Africans, furnishings for houses, food for owners, servants and slaves, the necessaries of domestic life, and all the machinery for growing crops, harvesting and preparing, and storing the end products for shipping to England.

William Wood wrote in 1718 that the trade in slaves was 'the spring and parent whence the others flow', and Sir Josiah Child wrote that, in his calculation, one man in the West Indies with ten African slaves, 'accounting what they eat, use and wear' gave work to four Englishmen.[6]

Wool had always been a major source of trade in Bristol. In the time of Edward II, the city had had its own wool staple, and the tomb of Thomas Blanket, a wool merchant, who is credited in local legend with inventing the length of woollen cloth that bears this name, can be found in the city church of St. Steven. It is therefore not surprising to find woollen goods (under the titles of 'serges', 'says', 'perpetuanos', 'arrangoes' and 'bays') on the ships' manifests of trade goods. 'Bridwater' cloth came from Bridgwater, and 'Welsh Plaines' from the West of England and Wales. Light woollen cloth was useful for trade on the African coast. Woollen garments were popular in the slave states of North America, where the climate favoured a thicker cloth in the winter. In the West Indies, woollen cloth was favoured because it was seen as being 'English' and so reinforced the desire of the fashionable in West Indian society to appear as English as possible.

Cotton was a better material for the colonies; and along with silk, it was the most popular as trade textile in Africa. One particularly successful item was an 'annabasse', a striped cotton loin-cloth. Since it was illegal to sell Indian cottons in England, they were re-exported (having come to England through the East India Company) to Africa, where different styles and qualities of cotton, 'brawls', 'tapsells', 'niccanees', 'cuttanees', 'buckshaws', 'nilias' and 'salempores', were all popular.

In the first quarter of the 17th century, Manchester expanded its cotton manufacture. Although they were not able to match the bright red, yellow and green Indian cloths that appealed to the Africans, they did make check fabrics that earned them a considerable share of the market that was to grow throughout the 18th century. Manchester cotton manufacture demonstrates the Triangular Trade in action. The cotton goods made in England – three quarters of which were manufactured from cotton produced on the plantations – would be bartered for Negroes in Africa, who in turn would end up working on the plantations.[7]

Earthenware goods were listed on ship's manifests, probably intended for the plantations rather than as trade goods. Bricks and tiles were also loaded on ships, providing the ballast for vessels on the West Indies run; they were then sold to the flourishing building industry.

Bristol provided a lot of the glass that was used in trade, in the form of mirrors and beads for Africa, and glass bottles (some containing local brewed beer, cider, perry and mineral water from the Hot-Well) for the colonies.[8] Because of the Africans' love of bright colours, the glass beads were manufactured in a wide variety of colours, as well as being patterned and gilded.

Metal goods were also in demand. These took the form of trade goods – iron and copper bars (one bar of iron was the equal of four of copper), pots, pans and kettles in copper and brass. The *Castle* of Bristol, sailing to Andony, Calebar in October 1727, listed the purchase of slaves with the equivalent cost in iron bars. Thus 3 women and 1 man cost the equivalent of 66 iron bars, which actually meant powder, muskets, beads, spirits, and copper rods. In the following month, still trading on the African coast, 3 men and 2 women cost 96.5 bars, which equated to 23 actual iron bars, 20 copper ones, 5 guns, 2 kegs of powder, 5 brawls (cotton cloths), 3 blue buffs (woollen cloths), 5 bunches of purple pipes (beads) and 5 Guinea cloths.[9]

Apart from metal bars, a variety of metal goods were also exported, both to Africa and the Colonies. Large metal 'bath pans' were sent particularly to the colonies – these had to be 'large to wash their bodies in'. Specific to Africa were the brass 'Guinea rods' and 'manelloes' or 'manillos', metal rings that resembled torque necklaces or bracelets. Bristol's Baptist Mills produced brass wire for trade with Africa.[10] An example of the variety of metal goods sent out to the colonies can be found in the inventory of the household goods lent by Mary Pinney, living in St John's Parish on Nevis, for the visit of 'His Excellency General Hart', taken in 1722:

Africans were living and working in Bristol as early as 1605. One of the daughters of Thomas Smyth and Florence Poulett of Ashton Court, with her African page boy. Circle of Gilbert Jackson, (c.1620-1640). (Christie's Images)

'…a silver teapot and lamp, 6 teaspoons, tongs and strainer; …a copper cistern weighing 9 lbs; …1 dozen ivory hafted knives and ditto of forks, ditto of ebony; 4 sugar knife and mallet; 2 pairs of snuffers and snuff dishes and 12 candlesticks; …4 spits, a frying pan, a pair of iron back weighing 37 lbs, 5 iron pots, 2 stew pans, a copper cullender, a copper coffee pot, a copper chocolate pot, 5 bell metal skillets, a brass kettle, a flesh fork, a scummer [skimmer], a brass ladle, and a bell metal mortar and pestle; …18 pewter plates, 2 soup dishes, a cheese plate weighing together 87 lbs, and 2 pewter basons…' [11]

Besides these manufacturing and domestic items, there were also the instruments of slavery – fetters, chains, padlocks, handcuffs, and branding irons. Captain W. Snelgrove wrote in 1754, 'When we purchase Negroes, we couple the sturdy Men together with Irons; but we suffer the Women and Children to go freely about: And soon after we have sail'd from the Coast, we undo all the Men's Irons.'[12] Another writer of the time made a slightly different report; he stated that it was common practice, 'to keep the Males apart from the Women and Children, to handcuff the former; Bristol Ships triple (link together in threes) such as are sturdy, with Chains round their Necks.'[13] The restraining of the slaves was to prevent mutiny or suicide attempts, and the branding irons were used to mark slaves for identification either by the ship on which they were to be transported or by different owners when it became time to sell them.

Guns were also highly sought-after; they fuelled the slave trade, as the local chieftains wanted guns so that they could make war on neighbouring tribes, thereby taking more captives who could be traded for goods, including more guns. The traders were not averse to playing on this demand to maintain an abundant supply of slaves. The bulk of these weapons were made in Birmingham, with some coming from London – a Birmingham gun could be traded for a Negro slave.[14]

The colonies also wanted metal goods – iron hoops for barrels, nails and wrought iron for building houses and working sheds, as well as the metal parts of sugar processing equipment.

Additional security to the English merchants who supplied the Triangular Trade came from the Navigation Laws of England. These forbade the colonists from using any shipping other than English, or buying any goods that had not originated from England. Their produce could only be exported in English ships, to England. In this way, all the wealth of the colonies flowed into English coffers – the Dutch, Scots and Irish were the principle maritime nations threatening this arrangement and against whom the laws were framed.

The port customs officials had the task of ensuring that all 'enumerated commodities' from the West Indies (including sugar, tobacco and timber) had come direct from the West Indies and not via a foreign port. They also had to ensure that

In 1765 John Pinney wrote: 'Since my Arrival I've purchased 9 Negroe Slaves at St Kitts and can assure you I was shock'd at the first appearance of human flesh expos'd for Sale. But Surely God ordain'd 'em for ye use and benefit of us: otherwise his Divine Will would have been made manifest by some particular sign or token.' Nevis by Nicholas Pocock (Bristol's Museums, Galleries & Archives)

the ship carrying the cargo was British or plantation-built, and that at least three-quarters of the crew were British – they therefore recorded the place of building, the ownership and tonnage of the ships they examined.[15] It was quite an undertaking; in 1709, for example, trade with the West Indies accounted for 10% of British mercantile shipping outside the British Isles.

When cargo was unloaded, it was moved to the owner's warehouse, or to one of the city buildings that could be rented. Non-perishable goods were sometimes left on the quayside for a time, usually with complaints of obstruction to the authorities. In all the records relating to the period of the slave trade, not one deals with the arrival of more than two slaves on any ship from the Triangular Trade (in 1715 Captain Nightingale left 'the proceeds of his two boys and girls, then on board his ship', in his will).[16] Even if all the eligible officers (captain, first mate, ship's doctor) retained their one or two privilege slaves on their journey back to Bristol, any ship could only bring back half a dozen people. Boatloads of slaves were never unloaded on the quayside, nor were they housed in any warehouse, shed, building or cave in the centre of the city.

With the expansion of shipping, new space had to be found for docking facilities. Alexander Pope, in 1739, described the centre of the city and the impact of shipping on it:

> '... in the middle of the streets, as far as you can see, hundreds of ships, their masts as thick as they can stand by one another ... This street is fuller of them than the Thames from London Bridge to Deptford, and at certain times only, the water rises to carry them out; so that, at other times, a long street, full of ships in the middle, and houses on both sides, looks like a dream'. [17]

Another aspect of the river was also noted by Pope:

> 'Next morning I went to the quay, but was very much surprised to find the river so very muddy...I can no better give a just idea of it than by a witty remark a young lady of my acquaintance made on her first seeing it, "that it seems as if Nature had taken a purge, and that was the operation". The filth and dirt that floats on the top makes it very loathsome.'

In 1720 the Merchant Venturers had purchased the Great Tower, part of the city's old defences, on Broad Quay and demolished it to provide extra room for shipping. By 1725, a number of specialist docks had been built – the Welsh Back had a wharf for corn and 'other goods out of market boats', whilst St. Augustine's Back had a quay for timber and naval stores.[18]

One trade that particularly flourished during this time of growth was that of ship-building. The more prominent shipbuilders were James Martin Hillhouse (whose company became Charles Hill & Co.) who had a yard close by Hotwells; Sydenham Teast and William Blannin at Wapping, and Richard Tombs at Dean's Marsh. If later records are anything to go by, there were a number of other lesser shipwrights also operating at the dockside.[19] Of the many ships built in the city, the majority were for general trading; slaves were loaded into ships that were not designed to carry people, let alone the numbers of Africans who were crammed into the holds. Later on, as trade developed and the rewards became greater, some English ships were built especially for transporting slaves. Those specifically for this trade aimed at producing maximum capacity whilst increasing speed - the quicker the time to cross the Atlantic, the fewer slaves would lose their lives and the greater would be the profit. Along with ship-building went the supplying of the vessels, with sails, rigging, paint, tar, oil, food and clothing for the crew, and so on.

Bristol involvement in the Africa trade was soon well established, but the London-based Africa Company had not released its stranglehold on the very lucrative and growing Africa trade without a fight. In 1711 the Company tried again to get their monopoly re-instated. The Corporation of Bristol, as well as the Merchant Venturers, immediately mounted a counter-attack. A series of deputations were sent to London, to lobby Parliament, and the Africa Company's attempt came to nothing.[20]

In 1711, thanks to the machinations of the Africa Company, the Council were forced to put up £100 to support the fight against the Company's attempts to regain their monopoly; during the next two years they paid a further £293 to John Day, a member of a prominent Bristol merchant family, to stay in London and keep an eye on things on Bristol's behalf. In 1713 the Company were obviously making a dangerous play for the monopoly. A petition was forwarded to the House of Commons by Bristol Corporation, in which the City set out its position on the trade in African goods, and slaves in particular. The document held that the City now depended largely on the trade with Africa and the West Indies. This related not only to in-coming goods, but to the building and fitting-out of ships, and the 'manufacture of wool, iron, tin, copper, brass &c., a considerable part whereof is exported to Africa for buying of Negroes.' These areas of trade were 'the great support of our people at home, and foundation of our trade abroad.' The Corporation requested forcefully that no single company, based in any one city, should ever be allowed sole trade with Africa; the Merchant Venturers added a similar declaration, adding that they had many vessels fit only for the Africa trade, whose exclusion would lead to their owners' ruin.[21]

In 1720 the South Sea Company, as part of its expansion plans, tried to resurrect a monopoly for itself in the African trade. Bristol Council once again leapt to the City's defence; they subscribed £140 towards fighting this new assault on their trading liberties. There was considerable jubilation, and vengeful exhortations against the Company to the House of Commons, when the 'South Sea Bubble' failed in the same year.[22]

On 12th May 1713 the Peace of Utrecht was declared by Dr. Robinson, Bishop of

Bristol, from the High Cross, St. Peter's Cross, Temple Cross, and other sites in the City. At last the War of the Spanish Succession with France, begun in 1702, was over, and the treaty saw Newfoundland, Nova Scotia, Hudson's Bay and part of the Island of St. Christopher ceded to England. The opening-up of British trade with Newfoundland, for example, meant that large quantities of salt fish (particularly the sub-standard type called Poor John) could be caught and processed for export to the West Indies, where it became part of the staple diet of the slaves. For Bristol, this increase in trade with Canada was very important as far as the city's trade was considered; another important element of the Peace was the Assiento Clause, whereby England was to hold the monopoly in supplying slaves to the Spanish colonies.[23] This trade was particularly valuable as the Spanish paid in gold and silver, rather than trade goods.

Unfortunately, this plan did not go as well as it should have done. Bristol, London and Liverpool rallied to provide increased supplies of Negroes after Assiento, to supply the Spanish colonies, but this was put in almost immediate jeopardy when a Spanish ship attacked a British one. The British navy retaliated and trade was disrupted for some years.

The Treaty of Assiento was followed by an attempt by the Government to arrange some form of free-trade agreement with France. This was opposed by various interests, particularly those involved in the spirit trade. The Bristol distillers had made a creditable brandy from apples during the war-time blockades, when French brandy was unavailable; they now saw this booming trade under threat. They were supported by the West Indies merchants who were using sugar to make rum, which could be drunk instead of French brandy – they, too, saw their trade suffering a possible reduction. The silk manufacturers were also against competitive French trade, while the clothiers wanted a ban on Spanish and Portuguese fabrics added to the French embargoes! As it turned out, the trade with France recovered anyway, and French brandy was available on sale in Bristol less than 15 years later.[24]

In 1721 George Benyon, a landing-waiter in the Customs House in Bristol, informed the East India Company that their rights were being infringed. Bristol ships, instead of heading for the West Coast of Africa, as they were supposed to, were going to Madagascar off the East Coast and trading there for slaves. The principal reason was that slaves could be bought on the island at a cheaper rate than on the Gold Coast. The East India Company were interested because any trade in the Indian Ocean infringed on their monopoly, and Madagascar was notorious as a centre for smuggling with India, which also cost them trade revenue. Further, the Company resented the fact that the Bristol ships were trading slaves for guns and goods, which were being smuggled back to India, and sold in direct competition with those being supplied by the Company itself.

On 2nd October, the Government issued an Order in Council, forbidding any private merchant to trade with Madagascar. Amongst the relevant papers is a note from the East India Company requesting that George Benyon should be promoted for

Broad Quay, Bristol School, c.1755, detail, with African pageboy. (Bristol's Museums, Galleries & Archives)

his zealousness. They also requested that he should be protected from the fury of the Bristol merchants who may have had their trade damaged – no idle request, given the lengths to which the merchants were prepared to go to protect their profits.

The matter might be seen as a storm in a teacup. However, in 1752 William Beckford, a wealthy Jamaica merchant, reported to the House of Commons:

'Many gentlemen here know that formerly the sugar colonies were supplied with Negroes from Madagascar, a vast island abounding with slaves, from whence the colonies drew large quantities till the East India Company interfered and prevented private traders from carrying on a commerce which they despised.'[25]

Between 1725 and 1731, the Africa Company made a number of further attempts to re-establish their monopoly, but they all failed. Even if these efforts were a hopeless rearguard action, they nevertheless cost Bristol mercantile interests some £2,000: of this sum, £900 was met by the Corporation. In the event, the Africa Company eventually abandoned the trade in slaves altogether, and concentrated on dealing in ivory and gold-dust, leaving the coast clear to Bristol ships.[26]

As an example, in October 1725, the ship *Dispatch*, owned by Isaac Hobhouse, Noblet Ruddock and William Baker, prominent Bristol merchants, was sent out on the Triangular Trade route. The account books for this voyage form part of the Hobhouse Papers, a collection of documents relating to Isaac Hobhouse & Co. who traded in the early 1700s (now housed in the Bristol Record Office). A list of the goods to be sent out for trade was given:

4,000 copper rods	*£251 12s 0d*
A quantity of cotton goods called Niccanees, Bejutas, Chints, Romalls, &c. [types of Indian cotton goods]	*£455 9s 6d*
A cask cowries [shells]	*£ 15 12s 4 1/2d*
2,000 Rangoes [arangoes – woollen cloths]	*£ 12 0s 0d*
206 cwt. iron bars, @ £19 per ton	*£196 1s 3 1/2d*
10 barrels gunpowder	*£ 40 17s 6d*
180 musquets @ 10/6 and chests	*£ 96 19s*
4 casks Monelas [manillas]	*£ 51 11s 9d*
4 1/2 cwt. Neptunes [copper pans]	*£ 38 0s 9 1/2d*
207 gals. brandy @ 2/6 and casks	*£ 28 1s 4 1/2d*
37 gals. cordial [gin] *@ 2/9*	*£ 5 3s 1 1/2d*
12 cwt. bugles [glass beads]	*£ 76 2s 10d*
18 fine hats edged with gold and silver, and 8 doz. felts edged with copper	*£ 21 4s*

The total value of the cargo was £1,330 8s 9 1/2d. The ship listed its provisions as:

40 cwt. of bread, 6 cwt. of flour, 66 1/2 cwt. of beef and pork, 190 bushels of beans and peas, 6 bushels of 'grutts' (groats – oat bran), 12 tierces and 4 hogsheads of ship beer.

The Captain, William Barry, was ordered to proceed to Andony, on the African coast. His instructions read:

> *'You must make the best of your way to the Coast of Africa that is to that part of it called Andony (without touching or tarrying at any other place) where you are to slave entirely … The Cargo of goods are of your own ordering, and as it is very good in kind and amounts to thirteen hundred and thirty pounds eight shillings and twopence farthing we hope it will purchase you 240 choice slaves, besides a quantity of teeth [ivory tusks] the latter of which are always to embrace provided they are large, seeing in that commodity there is no mortality to be feared'. In the event of buying slaves, they should be healthy young men, between the ages of 10 and 25 (a Nevis plantation owner wrote that slaves should be young, '...them full grown fellers think it hard to work never being brought up to it they take it to heart and dye or is never good for any thing ...' They were to be well fed, and not to be harmed by the crew, 'which has often been done to the prejudice of the voyage.'*

The *Dispatch* was then to proceed to Princess Island, just off the Gold Coast, and try to sell the slaves, if they would fetch '10 moidores' (Portuguese currency, worth £3 10s), and any of the remaining trade goods. If unsuccessful, the ship was to proceed to Antigua, then to Nevis or South Carolina, in order to off-load their cargo. In these early years, slaves were the least popular African cargo, as they were liable to illness and death – therefore, they tended to be carried if no other trade goods were available. Of course, as the demand for slaves grew, so the trade in human beings rose in importance and volume.

As an incentive to keep the slaves healthy, Captain Barry was allowed 4% commission on the 'net proceeds of the live cargo'. In addition, he was permitted to select two slaves who he would buy from the cargo at an agreed price. He could then sell them on in the West Indies, or bring them back to England. The Chief Mate and the Surgeon or Doctor was also allowed two slaves, but, unlike the Captain, they had to pay for their slaves' food on the voyage.[27]

The biggest problem in shipping people, whether African slaves, British bond-servants or free passengers, was that the crowded and unsanitary conditions on board the small ships of the 18th century, meant there was always a risk of epidemic illness. The *Castle* of Bristol, sailing from Andony, Calebar in 1727, reported the loss of 32 of a cargo of 271 slaves to dysentery, 'apoplexy' and 'pleuritick fever'.[28] Most ships carried a doctor, whose job was the take care of crew and slaves. In particular, he was to screen the slaves as they were embarked and it was hoped that he could identify those with possible epidemic diseases, so allowing only a healthy cargo to be loaded. Unfortunately, the doctor was not always successful; as one ship's captain noted on one voyage, 'What the smallpox spar'd, the flux swept off to our great regret.'[29]

In an attempt to keep the slaves healthy, some ships carried musicians. Rather than to raise the spirits, they were to provide music for the slaves to 'dance' to, thereby giving them exercise on the deck of the ship. The *Castle*, in 1729, carried a piper, a fiddler and a drummer.[30]

The growth in the volume of the slave trade may be read into the instruction given Captain Barry. Another Bristol ship was about to leave on the same venture, and the Captain was advised to make all haste, in order to 'see that he is not outdone in slaving by other commanders.'

Captain Barry, like other captains of the period, was 'recommended to Good God's almighty protection'. He went on to sign his orders, and added that he would follow them, 'God willing'. The traders and transporters of slaves in the 18th century saw no incongruity in appealing to God to aid their endeavours. One of the reasons given for trading Africans in the first place was that they would benefit from the advantage of being in direct contact with Christianity, rescued from their 'heathen' religion.[31]

In the *Gentleman's Magazine* of July 1740, a subscriber, signing himself *Mercator Honestus*, asked for some 'wise and good men' to explain to him the justification for enslaving one's fellow men. The answer came:

> *'The inhabitants of Guinea are indeed in a most deplorable State of Slavery, under the arbitrary Powers of their Princes both as to Life and Property ... by purchasing, or rather ransoming the Negroes from their national Tyrants, and transplanting them under the benign influences of the Law, and Gospel, they are advanced to much greater Degrees of Felicity, tho' not to absolute Liberty ...'* [32]

However, Daniel Defoe, in his *Reformation of Manners* (1702) wrote:

> *'The harmless Natives basely they trepan*
> *And barter Baubles for the Souls of Men.*
> *The Wretches they to Christian Climes bring o'er*
> *To serve worse Heathen than they did before.'* [33]

The MP Temple Luttrell also gave a further, more honest reason for English slave trading:

> *'Some gentlemen may, indeed, object to the slave trade as inhuman and impious; let us consider that if our colonies are to be maintained and cultivated, which can only be done by African Negroes, it is surely better to supply ourselves with those labourers in British bottoms [ships], than purchase them through the medium of French, Dutch or Danish factors.'* [34]

A rumour arose amongst Africans that embracing Christianity meant that the

'Christian' slave would become free. In 1729 the Attorney General, Sir Philip Yorke, and the Solicitor-General, Mr. Talbot, ruled that being baptised into the Christian Church did not confer freedom or in any way alter the conditions of slavery. He further added that merely by coming to England, a slave did not automatically become free. The ruling read:

> *'We are of the opinion, that a Slave by coming from the West Indies to Great Britain or Ireland either with or without his master, doth not become free; and that his Master's Property or Right in him is not thereby determined or varied; and that Baptism doth not bestow freedom on him, nor make any Alteration in his Temporal Condition in these Kingdoms. We are also of opinion, that his Master may legally compel him to return again to the Plantations.'* [35]

The profit on trading slaves may be ascertained from the voyage of the Castle, in 1727, where 271 slaves were loaded for the West Indies, having been bartered for goods worth £2 15s per head. The following year, the agent John Jones wrote to his uncle and employer, Isaac Hobhouse, from Jamaica. The Virgin from the Gold Coast had arrived with a cargo of 262 slaves, 'and they come at £30 17s 6d per head round, which is a good price considering there was so many small among them ... The demand for Negroes continues; there is now 500 in harbour and all bought up.' Despite an annual import of about 30,000 Africans in the decades of the early 18th century, there was always a demand for more. In February 1730, Mr. R. Assheton of Tyndall, Assheton & Co., wrote to Isaac Hobhouse, 'Surely Negroes were never so much wanted, nor can that want be supplied for two years to come, which the Days (Bristol merchants) are very sensible of, and push all they can. The general terms Pratten buys at is £30 to £32 per head for men, women, boys, and girls.' Assheton was able to report in a later letter that a cargo of 234 slaves had all sold for £35 a head. [36]

Even a sick cargo could make a profit. In 1730 the *Freke* galley, owned by William Freke & Co., Merchants of Bristol, arrived in Barbados with a cargo of 141 men, 75 women, 65 boys and 48 girls from Guinea. Although many of them were ill, the men fetched between £22 and £29, although a few sold for as little as £2 10s. The women sold for about £23, except for two who fetched only 15s each. The children cost about £14 each. In total, the 329 people fetched £6,207. After the Agent had taken out his commission of £460 6s 9d, including import duty of 5s a head and £25 9s 'for treating customers during the sale', the total profit on the sale of even 'an indifferent cargo' was £5,746 18s 3d. [37]

In 1729 Mr. Assheton had written to Mr. Hobhouse of another, less profitable venture. A cargo of slaves had fetched only £19 10s a head, due to their being mostly too old or too young ; of those sold, many died within a few weeks, but this was just bad luck for the purchasers. (the Agent in Kingston wrote to his principal, 'The people of Bristol seem doubtful of the Jamaica Market for Slaves, I think the worst

Cargo since I've been here is the *Aurora*, & they turn out at about £19 10s round, & is the best Sale I've been concerned in, they were in general either Children or Greyheaded...').[38]

The Captain of the *Greyhound*, in the same year, wrote to Hobhouse of a disastrous voyage; he had taken 339 slaves at Bonny, but had lost 125 on the Atlantic run. The remaining 214 were so sick that they fetched only £20 each. This was not as bad as the voyage described by the Jamaica agent to Isaac Hobhouse and his partner in this particular venture, Onesiphorus Tyndall; two-fifths of the slaves had died during the voyage, more died on landing, and of those who survived, many were almost worthless.[39]

Sickness was not the only reason for loss of cargo. In 1694 Thomas Phillips, Master of the *Hannibal*, noted in his journal:

> 'The Negroes are so wilful and loth to leave their own country, that they have often leap'd out of the canoes, boat or ship, into the sea, and kept under water until they were drowned... They have a more dreadful apprehension of Barbados than we can of hell, tho' in reality they live much better there than in their own country; but home is home, etc; we have likewise seen divers of them eaten by sharks, of which a prodigious number kept about the ships in this place, and I have been told will follow her hence to Barbados, for the dead Negroes that are thrown over-board in the passage... We had about 12 Negroes did wilfully drown themselves, and others starv'd themselves to death; for 'tis their belief that when they die they return home to their own country and friends again...'[40]

In 1736 the ship *Prince of Orange* was proceeding to the West Indies from Africa, when:

> '...a hundred of the men slaves jumped overboard, and it was with great difficulty we saved as many as we did. We lost 33 ... who were resolved to die. Some others have died since, but not to the owner's loss, they being sold before any discovery was made of the injury the salt water had done them. The Captain has lost two of his own slaves.'[41]

Another very occasional hazard was rebellion amongst the slaves themselves. In the *Gloucester Journal* of 28th January 1729 a letter from Bristol gave '...the melancholy news that Captain Holliday with all his crew except the cabin boy, have been murdered on the coast of Africa by the Negroes.' A different disaster overtook the *Callabar Merchant* out of Bristol, which was seized by pirates on leaving the African coast in 1719. The ship was held for nine weeks, after which it was released with only about half its cargo of 156 slaves (the pirates took the rest). By the time they arrived in Virginia, 36 more had died of illness.[42] Pirates, corsairs and privateers could all prove hazardous to shipping on the triangular route. During the War of the Spanish Succession (1702-1712), for example, a number of Bristol ships trading with Africa were seized as prizes by French and Spanish privateers.

After successful voyages, the ship's officers, captain, chief mate and surgeon could all bring Africans to Bristol as their preference slaves. On a successful voyage, a captain could make a handsome profit, as well as his normal wages, and some of the captains undoubtedly lived in some luxury. They might well keep their slaves in attendance during their time on shore, perhaps selling them on when a new voyage came along. In this way, wealthy Bristol families could acquire black servants without direct contact with the West Indies or the Africa Trade.

During the first third of the century, some of the church records of the births, marriages and deaths of Negro slaves refer to their owners as captains. In January 1723, at St. Philip & St. Jacob, a black servant of Captain Jacob Smith, named Thomas Jamaica, was baptised; in January 1725 the burial was recorded of that same Thomas Jamaica, 'Captain Jacob Smith's black, a Christian Negro'. In November 1728 in the same church, the baptism took place of William Gloucester, 'Captain Martin's black'. Another baptism was that of Alexander, at St. Augustine the Less in October 1730, who belonged to Captain Thomas Edwards.[43] Captain Day had a rather more difficult problem with his slave, Richard Cornwall. In the *Gloucester Journal* of February and April 1737 an interesting case was reported:

> *'Last Sunday one Sarah Elliott was committed to Newgate for endeav-ouring to extort money from one Richard Cornwall, a Christian Negro servant to Captain Day in College Green, under pretence that she had a child by him and which was then alive in Berkeley in Gloucestershire. The Black insisted on seeing the child before he would condescend to her demand and told her that if it was his child he should know it by the colour of the skin. The woman, artfully to deceive the fellow, procured a borrowed child with its skin smutted over, but he, calling for a wet napkin and rubbing the child's face, found it a fair complexion...'*

Sarah failed, and was sentenced to the pillory. Her attempt to extort money from Richard or his owner for child maintenance was unsuccessful.[44]

Another route whereby Africans arrived in Bristol was as the servants of merchants and plantation owners from the West Indies who returned to Bristol, either to visit or to retire; an agent on Barbados wrote in 1689 : 'By a kind of magnetic force England draws to it all that is good in the plantations. It is the centre to which all things tend. Nothing but England can we relish or fancy; our hearts are here, wherever our bodies be.' In August 1703 the records of St. Stephen's Church give details of the marriage of Joseph Thompson and Mary Columbus, both described as Negroes, 'of Jamaica and Bristol'. The bride and groom were both the 'servants of Merchant Heathcoat, a Sojourner in the Parish of St. Stephen in Bristol'.[45]

The majority of African slaves in Bristol seem to have ended up in domestic service. In July 1715 St. Augustine the Less carried the record of the baptism of Cathrin, 'a black maid of Mr. Watkin's'.[46] In September of the same year, at St. Thomas's, Hannah was also baptised, described as the 'nigro [sic] servant of Mr. Richard Lathrop, about 8 years old'. In January 1729 at Temple Church, Noah was buried, 'a black boy, about 5 years old and servant to Mr. Richard Eagles'. In December 1734 Sabina, 'a black maid of Mrs. Round's', was baptised at St. Philip & St. Jacob, and another baptism took place at Holy Trinity, Stapleton, in February 1737 of James Pitman, 'a Black, Servant to Mr. Scandrett'.[47]

The merchants of Bristol were not only the driving force behind the African slave trade, their ranks provided the mayors, sheriffs, aldermen, Merchant Venturers, Members of Parliament and Council officials of the 18th century. Far from being monsters of inhumanity, they were perceived, in their day, as honest, virtuous, god-fearing, family men. Some believed that the African people were a lesser people and born to be slaves of a greater people (Europeans). Some believed they were better off for being introduced to Christianity, even if they were slaves. It was thought that if God had objected to slavery, He would undoubtedly have let His feelings be known. John Pinney summed the attitude up in a letter written from Nevis in 1765:

> 'Since my Arrival I've purchased 9 Negroe Slaves at St Kitts and can assure you I was shock'd at the first appearance of human flesh exposed for Sale. But Surely God ordain'd 'em for ye use and benefit of us: otherwise his Divine Will would have been made manifest by some particular sign or token.' [48]

In fact, many of the merchants never saw any Negroes other than the few nurses, maids and valets of their friends, who seemed fit, well-treated and content. They had no real understanding of the cruelty and barbarism being practised throughout the Triangular Trade in the Americas and West Indies.

The 'companies' trading in slaves often comprised several individual traders, sometimes as many as eight. These men would purchase a ship, pay for supplies and a trade cargo, and settle the crew's wages. In return they would share any net profit on the return of the ship. Some smaller traders might be interested in only one voyage; other, larger concerns could be involved in several trips each year, and could reap rich rewards as a result. Their ships sailed for what was called the 'Guinea Coast', which covered Gambia, Sierra Leone, the Windward Coast, Anamabo, Whyday, New Calebar, Bonny and Old Calebar – in fact, most of the African coast from Cape Verde to the Congo.

The Bristol Record Society has produced a series of volumes, edited by Patrick McGrath and Elizabeth Ralph, on the ships that plied the triangular trade in the 18th century. These books give details of their tonnage, the size of the crew, names of the master and owner(s), the dates of departure and return, the ports visited, and the

*Bristol docks looking towards St Mary Redcliffe. Nicholas Pocock
(Bristol's Museums, Galleries & Archives)*

number of slaves transported (where this information is given). Sometimes other elements of information are available in the records, which add to the picture of the slave trade during this century.

A large number of Bristol merchants organised voyages to buy slaves, but a small group seems to have dominated the trade between 1698 and 1729. James Day led the field with 38 voyages, while his brother Peter Day added another 13. Noblet Ruddock (one of the three owners of the dispatch, see above) sent ships on 30 trips, John Becher backed 27, Richard Henvill 24, Abraham Hooke 23, John Duckinfield 21, and William Jefferis 20 – his brother Joseph provided a further 11 voyages to the family business. These men were known as Agents, who took responsibility for the cargo, for all financial matters and for distributing profits at the end. In all, about 19 agents were responsible for 60% of all slaving trips from 1698 until 1729.[49]

Some of these agents, like the Jefferis brothers, Thomas Freke and Francis Rogers, were members of established Bristol merchant families. Others, like the Days, Duckinfield and Henvill, were related by marriage or apprenticeship to these great Houses. A few, like Abraham Hooke, were the sons of local tradesmen, who established their fortunes by their involvement in this venture. Most of them were involved in other businesses beyond the Africa Trade; Noblet Ruddock financed trading ventures in Ireland and Europe, whilst Isaac Hobhouse was a partner in a local copper company.

It was not wholly a story of financial success. Noblet Ruddock went bankrupt in 1726. By 1730 he was on record as being a slave factor in Barbados, so that he did not completely lose his connection with the trade.[50] There were great fortunes to be made, and a man did not have to be a merchant to benefit from the profits of the slave trade. Few men had sufficient funds to finance several voyages a year so the new banking institutions became essential to the smooth running of the trade in Bristol. Some slave traders themselves moved into the more lucrative field of banking. The first official bank in Bristol was opened on 1 August 1750, known as The Old Bank, at 42 Broad Street. The first partners were Onesiphorus Tyndall, Harford Lloyd, Isaac Elton, William Miller, Thomas Knox and Matthew Hale. Tyndall was a West Indian merchant and partner in a company of drysalters. Lloyd was also a merchant, living at 1 Dighton Street, later known as Harford House (his grand-daughter Mary Beck married Charles Harford). The first clients of the Old Bank were Israel Alleyne, John Braikenridge, Samuel Bright, Isaac Burges, Nehemiah Champion II, William Champion & Co, Thomas Curtis (Mayor 1749), Mark Davis, John Evans & Co, Richard Farr (Mayor 1763), Robert Gordon (Mayor 1773), William Gordon, George Hale, Henry Hobhouse, James Laroche (Mayor 1750), Nicholas Perry, William Swymmer and Henry Weare; by the following year they were joined by John Brickdale, Charles Bragge, John Curtis, Thomas Daniel, Thomas Deane (Mayor 1770), George Daubeny, Sir Abraham Elton (3rd Bart.), Ann Farley, William Gayner, Thomas Goldney, Richard Prankard, John Scandrett and Sir Bouchier Wrey Bart. Many of the patrons of the bank were involved in the slave trade or had West Indian interests.[51]

Perhaps the most famous record of a Bristol slave is the tombstone in Henbury churchyard, to Scipio Africanus. It reads:

> 'Here lieth the Body of Scipio Africanus Negro Servant to ye Right Honourable Charles William Earl of Suffolk and Bradon who died ye 21 December 1720 aged 18 years':

> 'I who was born a PAGAN and a SLAVE
> Now sweetly sleep a CHRISTIAN in my Grave
> What tho' my hue was dark my SAVIOURS sight
> Shall change this darkness into radiant Light
> Such grace to me my Lord on earth has given
> To recommend me to my Lord in Heaven
> Whose glorious second coming here I wait
> With Saints and Angels him to celebrate'

Apart from the headstone, little is known of Scipio. His mistress was Arabella Astry, one of the heiresses of Sir Samuel Astry and his wife, Elizabeth Morse. Arabella was 25 when in 1715 she married Charles William Howard Lord Waldon who, within 3 years, was Earl of Suffolk and Bindon, and the owner of Scipio. The couple passed their time between their two houses, his at Audley End near London and hers at Henbury, Bristol. Scipio died at Henbury in December 1720, Charles in February 1721 and Arabella in June 1722.

It is impossible to know where Scipio came from, whether he belonged to Charles or Arabella, whether he came into England through London or Bristol. There is one interesting possibility. Given that the Earl and his servant died so close to one another, it might be that they were victims of the same contagious disease. Since it is not possible to check every location where they might have contracted the disease, if there was one, it would be reasonable to examine the church records at Henbury to see if there were any contagious diseases ravaging the parish at the time. No epidemics appeared to be raging; between March 1717 and April 1721, the maximum number of adult deaths in any single month was four, and quite often it was one or none. In the month that the Earl died he was one of only three adults.

However, the register of baptisms shows one anomaly, in April 1720, 8 months before Scipio died. The usual entry in the register takes the form, 'Mary daughter of John Smith and of Jane his wife', or 'James son of John and Jane Smith'. Occasionally it reads, 'James the base child of Jane Smith'. On the 24 April 1720 there is a single entry, 'Josph Williams capt.' This suggests that either Joseph was an adult, or the names of his parents were not known. However, the term 'capt' may be a contraction of Captain, or the Latin, 'captus', a captive or slave. Since one of the things we know about Scipio is that he had been baptised, this could be the first appearance of the African slave who was to be buried as Scipio Africanus, so loved by the Earl and Countess that the exceptional sum of two guineas was spent on his lavish tombstone.[52]

Not all slaves were valued or acquiescent members of a household. Almost from the beginning of the century, slaves were escaping from captivity in Bristol. These escapes were referred to as 'elopements', and several of them were reported in the local papers, accompanied by a description of the absent slave, and the offer of a reward for their re-capture. Given that these escapes started during the early years of the trade, long before abolition was widely talked of and before there was a widespread and vocal opposition to slavery, the men in question showed enormous courage and ingenuity. They might hope to travel to another port and sign on as a sailor, or to lose themselves in a large, anonymous city like London, where their presence was occasionally officially noted amongst the poor.

It is hardly remarkable that the majority of runaways belonged to captains – Foye, Courtney, Eaton, Bouchier, Nash and Holbrook all took out advertisements about 'eloping' slaves. If the captain was planning to sell his slave before leaving Bristol on his next voyage, and particularly if he planned to ship the slave to the West Indies for sale, this would explain the high percentage of captain's slaves that absconded. Slaves were aware of the difference in attitude to slaves in England as opposed to the Indies, where vicious cruelty was part of slave ownership. With the white slave-owning population out-numbered by the slaves, it was believed that order could only be kept by excessive repression and cruelty.

The earliest recorded absconding was in the *London Journal* of January 1713. Captain Foye of Bristol offered a reward of £5 for the return of 'a Negro called Scipio (his Negro name Ossion), of middle stature, aged about 24, speaks imperfect English, somewhat splayfooted.' In July 1715 Mr. Pyne, the Bristol postmaster (who was legally responsible for the retrieval of runaway slaves), offered 2 guineas and expenses to anyone who should re-capture Captain Stephen Courtney's slave, who was about 20, 'having 3 or 4 marks on each temple and the same on each cheek.'[53]

Scipio seems to have been a popular name for slaves. The original owner of the name had been a Roman general, called Africanus because of his successful African campaigns, and it obviously seemed a fitting name for an African. Apart from Scipio Africanus, buried at Henbury, and Captain Foye's servant, Scipio, a man called Edward Peter Scipio was buried in St. Andrews Church in May 1730.[54] A child called Mary Scipio was buried at St. Michael's Church in October 1750.[55]

The local papers also took advertisements for the sale of individual slaves. In August 1723, *Farley's Bristol Journal* carried an advertisement from Captain John Gwythen, offering for sale 'a Negro man about 20 years, well limb'd, fit to serve a gentleman or to be instructed in a trade.'

The names given to African slaves varied considerably, from the imaginative to the ordinary. One of the earliest recorded instances of an African with an English name was Joan Smyth, buried in 1603. Other slaves included Ann Jones and Adam Arthur (baptised in 1704 and 1705 respectively, in Temple Church).[56] Then there were John

The majority of African slaves in Bristol ended up in domestic service. Prospect of Bristol, 1734, by S & N Buck, with African pageboy in the foreground. (Bristol's Museums, Galleries & Archives)

Middleton (baptised in St. Michael's Church in 1720), Thomas Smith (baptised at St. Stephen's Church in 1721) and Catherine Smith (buried in St. Stephen's in 1724). Other examples were Robert Harley (baptised at St. Nicholas in 1729) and Benjamin Cambridge, whose son, John, was buried at St. Augustine's in February 1738.[57]

An English-named family of slaves attended St. Augustine the Less in the city centre. In September 1725, Rebecca, the servant of Mr. Neale, was baptised there. In September 1728, she married William Rice; they are both described in the record as black. Their first daughter, Mary, was baptised in March 1731, followed by Betty in April 1733, and Susannah in August 1735. Tragedy struck the family in January 1737 with the death of 6-year-old Mary; however, in October of that year, Rebecca had another daughter, also christened Mary.[58]

There were several slaves given the surname Bristol – William (baptised at St. Augustine's in 1693), John, servant to Captain Harman (baptised at St. Andrews in November 1744),[59] and another William (baptised at St. Augustine the Less in December 1757).[60] Some names were given in a supposedly humorous spirit or because of some association known only to the person who gave the name. These included Becher Fleming's boy, Tallow, who was left in his will to Mrs Mary Becher in 1718 (Fleming's will has him 'late of the Island of Jamaica, but now of the City of Bristol'),[61] and a gingerbread maker called Commodore, who married a 'single woman of the same parish' called Venus, at St. Michael's Church in September 1721.[62] A slave called Neptune was buried at St. Andrew's Church in September 1749.[63]

A few Africans retained their own names. The Coromanti, a tribe from the Gold Coast, sometimes named their children for the day of the week on which they were born:

	Male	Female
Monday	Cudjo	Juba
Tuesday	Cubbenhah	Beneba
Wednesday	Quaco	Cuba
Thursday	Quaw	Abba
Friday	Cuffee	Phibba
Saturday	Quamin	Mimba
Sunday	Quashy	Quasheba

The earliest reference to a Coromanti in Bristol is in July 1704, when George, the son of George Belford and his wife, Benebo, was baptised at St. John the Baptist Church – Beneba is the name for a Coromanti female born on Tuesday. In 1720 a Sarah Quashabrack was baptised at St. Stephen's – a girl born on Sunday would be called Quasheba. Thomas Quaco was buried at St. Augustine the Less in March 1735 – Quaco is the name of a male born on Wednesday. Incidentally, in July of the same year, Thomas, son of Thomas and Phillis Quaco, was baptised at the same church,

'I who was born a PAGAN and a SLAVE
Now sweetly sleep a CHRISTIAN in my Grave…'

The most famous record of a Bristol slave are the tombstones in Henbury churchyard, Bristol, to
Scipio Africanus. (M.Manson)

probably the posthumous son of the late Thomas Quaco who died in March; a Phillis Quaco died in September 1740.[64]

In December 1747 John Coffee was baptised at Bristol Cathedral. This may be a name that reflects the coffee-colour of his skin, the produce of the plantation on which he worked, or may refer to his having been a Coromanti born on Friday – this would be the Anglicised version of the name Cuffee. In *Felix Farley's Journal* of July 1769 there is an account of one Henry Coffee, committed to Newgate on a charge of stealing iron hoops from a hooper, Mr. Lucas. A second generation Coromanti may be Harriet Quyman, baptised at St. James's in February 1785; her surname, Quamin, could indicate a male born on Saturday, possibly a reference to her father. One of the latest references, not long before slavery was declared illegal, is to a Joseph Cudjoe, buried at St. Mary Redcliffe in February 1803 – Cudjo is a male born on Monday.[66]

The strength, resilience and intelligence of the Coromanti may be clearly seen in an advertisement that appeared in the *Kingston Daily Advertiser*, Jamaica on 7 June 1790:

> 'Absconded from John Munro's wharf at this place, the 30th ultimo, a Negro Sailor Man, of the Coromantee nation: he is about 5 feet 5 inches high, his face is furrowed with small pox marks, he has no brand mark, his back has got several lumps which in some manner resemble a bunch of grapes…he is artful, speaks the English, French, Dutch, Danish and Portuguese languages; of course it is thought he may endeavour to pass for a free man.' [67]

Having survived enslavement, smallpox and back injuries, this man was able to plan and execute an escape, aided by his knowledge of at least five European languages. Bryan Edwards wrote a *History…of the British Colonies in the West Indies*, published in 1801. Concerning the Coromanti, he had this to say:

> 'The circumstances which distinguish the Koromantyn, or Gold Coast, Negroes, from all others, are firmness both of body and mind; a ferociousness of disposition; but withal, activity, courage, and a stubbornness, or what an ancient Roman would have deemed an elevation of soul, which prompts them to enterprises of difficulty and danger; and enables them to meet death, in its most horrible shape, with fortitude or indifference.' [68]

In 1694 Thomas Phillips, master of the *Hannibal*, wrote in his journal:

> 'The Negroes most in demand at Barbados are the gold coast, or, as they call them, Coramantines, which will yield 3 or 4 pounds a head more than the Whidaws, or, as they call them, Papa Negroes, but these are preferred before the Angola, as they are before the Alampo, which are accounted the worst of all.' [69]

Notes

1 Richardson, David, *Bristol, Africa and the 18th Century Slave Trade to America: Years of Ascendancy 1730-1745*, Vol.2 (1987), p.27.
2 Minchinton, Walter, *'The Port of Bristol in the Eighteenth Century'*, McGrath, Patrick (ed.), *Bristol in the Eighteenth Century* (1972), p.128 and Bristol and its Environs (1875), p.261.
3 Marcy, Peter T, *Eighteenth Century Views of Bristol and Bristolians*, McGrath, Patrick (ed.), *Bristol in the Eighteenth Century* (1972), p.14.
4 *Bristol in the Eighteenth Century*, op cit. p.14
5 Minchinton, Walter, *'The Port of Bristol in the Eighteenth Century'*, McGrath, Patrick (ed.), *Bristol in the Eighteenth Century* (1972), p.129
6 Williams, Eric, *Capitalism and Slavery* (1975), p.52
7 Williams, Eric, op cit (1975), p.68-70
8 Minchinton, Walter, *'The Port of Bristol in the Eighteenth Century'*, McGrath, Patrick (ed.), *Bristol in the Eighteenth Century* (1972), p.133
9 John Taylor, *A Book About Bristol* (1872), p.329
10 Williams, Eric, op cit, p.83
11 Pares, Richard, *A West-Indian Fortune* (1968), p.337-9
12 Craton, Michael, Walvin, James & Wright, Davis, Slavery, *Abolition and Emancipation* (1976), p.43
13 McInnes, CM, *'Bristol and the Slave Trade'*, McGarth, Patrick (ed.), *Bristol in the Eighteenth Century* (1972), p.175-6
14 Williams, Eric, op cit, p.82
15 Minchinton, Walter, *'The Port of Bristol in the Eighteenth Century'*, McGrath, Patrick (ed.), *Bristol in the Eighteenth Century* (1972), p.146]
16 Latimer, John, *The Annals of Bristol in the Eighteenth Century* (1970), p.15
17 Marcy, Peter T, *'Eighteenth Century Views of Bristol and Bristolians'*, McGrath,
18 Patrick (ed.), *Bristol in the Eighteenth Century* (1972), p.20]
19 Minchinton, Walter, *'The Port of Bristol in the Eighteenth Century'*, McGrath, Patrick (ed.), *Bristol in the Eighteenth Century* (1972), p.153
20 Minchinton, Walter, *'The Port of Bristol in the Eighteenth Century'*, McGrath, Patrick (ed.), *Bristol in the Eighteenth Century* (1972), p.134]
21 Latimer, John, *The Annals of Bristol in the Eighteenth Century* (1970), p.89
22 Latimer, John, op cit, p.89-90
23 ibid, p.90
26 ibid, p.100
27 ibid p.101
28 ibid, p.127-8
29 ibid, p.90
30 ibid, p.142-6
31 John Taylor, opcit, p.329
32 Walvin, James, *Slavery and the Slave Trade* (1983), p.54
33 Latimer, John, op cit, p.146
34 ibid, p.144
35 Plimmer, Charlotte & Denis, *Slavery, The Anglo-American Involvement* (1973), p.45-7
36 Plimmer, Charlotte & Denis, op cit, p.11]
37 House of Commons Proceedings (1777), 19, Coll.305
38 Craton, Michael, Walkvin, James & Wright, David, op cit, p.165
39 Latimer, John, op cit, p.144
40 ibid, p.145
41 McInnes, CM, *'Bristol and the Slave Trade'*, McGarth, Patrick (ed.), *Bristol in the Eighteenth Century* (1972), p.177]
42 Latimer, John, op cit, p.145
43 Plimmer, Charlotte & Denis, op cit, p.27
44 Richardson, David, op cit, p.75
45 McGrath, Patrick, Ralph, Elizabeth (eds.), *Bristol, Africa and the 18th Century Slave Trade to America*, Vol. I (1986), p.81
46 Bristol Record Office, FC/StP&J/R/1, FCP/StAug/R/1
47 Lindegaard, D.P., op cit, p.17
48 Bristol Record Office, FCP/StS/R/1
49 Bristol Record Office RO, FCP/StAug/R/1]
50 Lindegaard, DP, op cit, p.23, 32, 37, 33]

51   McInnes, CM, *'Bristol and the Slave Trade'*, McGarth, Patrick (ed.), *Bristol in the Eighteenth Century* (1972), p.177]

52   Richardson, David, Bristol, *Africa and the 18th Century Slave Trade to America: Years of Expansion* 1698-1729 Vol.1 (1986), p.xxii

53   Richardson, David, Bristol, *Africa and the 18th Century Slave Trade to America: Years of Expansion 1698-1729* Vol.1 (1986), p.xxii-xxiii

54   Cave, Charles Henry, *A History of Banking in Bristol 1750-1899* (1899), p.41-6

55   Bristol Record Office, *Church Records for St Mary's; Astry Papers, receipt*

56   Latimer, John, op cit, p.146-7

57   BRO, FCP/StA/R/1

58   Lindegaard, DP, op cit, p.39

59   ibid p.26, 9]

60   BRO, FCP/StM/R/1, FCP/StS/R/1, FCP/StN/R/1

61   BRO, FCP/StAug/R/1

62   Lindegaard, DP, op cit, p.12-3

63   BRO, FCP/StAug/R/1

64   Lindegaard, D.P., op cit, p.41

65   ibid.17, 41

66   BRO, FCP/StA/R/1

67   Lindegaard, DP, op cit, p.6

68   C Roy Huddleston (ed), *The Bristol Cathedral Register* (1933), p.3]

69   Lindegaard, op cit, p.36, 18

70   Walvin, James, op cit, (1983), p.109]

71   Craton, Michael, Walvin, James & Wright, David, op cit, p.131

72   Plimmer, Charlotte & Denis, op cit, p.27

FOUR

While Britain was trading African slaves to her colonies, slave trading between other parties was also being recorded in Bristol. In 1734 Captain Philip Graves of the Bristol ship *Ferdinand* had a letter published in the *London Journal*. He appealed to a (un-named) Bristol merchant for financial help in ransoming himself and his 7-man crew, as well as the crews of three other ships that were in his convoy, from a Moroccan prison. The Admiral of Sallee had seized their ships, and the men could be bought back by making payment to a middleman in Gibraltar who traded with Sallee on the Barbary Coast. If the ransom was not forthcoming, the men would be sold into slavery.[1]

During the 16th and 17th centuries, Bristol did not trade only in people enslaved from Africa. In 1705 Robert Beverley of Virginia wrote concerning the differences between the Africans and their British bond-servant contemporaries:

> *'Slaves are the Negroes and their posterity, following the condition of the mother ... They are called slave in respect of the time of their servitude because it is for life. Servants are those which serve only for a few years, according to the time of their indenture, or the custom of their country'.*[2]

Yet the trade in bond-servants was, in some instances, little better than slavery. They might be willing to trade their labour; many, however, were convicted criminals. In 1718 a law was introduced that allowed transportation as an alternative to the death sentence. Each local authority was responsible for shipping its own convicted felons to the colonies for the fixed term of their sentence. The standard penalty was seven years service for a youth and four years for an adult. Ship's captains were paid to transport them. In 1727, a prominent Bristol merchant and slave trader, William Jefferis (who would go on to be Mayor in 1738) received 12 guineas for transporting four prisoners on one of his ships.[3]

The bond-servant's services were sold at the end of the voyage. In 1729, according to one of the Hobhouse letters, 12 'servants' were sold for between £13 and £30 at Jamaica.[4] This profit meant that not all the 'servants' on sale were, in fact, condemned criminals. Some were young people who had been tricked into leaving England for what they thought were well-paid jobs in the colonies, with a chance to make their fortunes. Others were genuinely seeking a new life in a new country, and used this means of making a journey that they would otherwise have been unable to afford. The New York Gazette, 10 May 1774, reported the arrival of 'servants' including weavers, tailors, blacksmiths, masons, joiners and spinsters 'from 14 to 35 years of age' These bond-servants were sold for £15 each. In 1793, William Cobbett wrote that he had observed people 'sold like cattle' at Wilmington; a seven-year-old girl was offered to serve until she was 21, for the price of six guineas.[5]

Others were blatantly kidnapped. In March 1729, as reported in the Gloucester Journal, a water bailiff was sent by a Bristol court to rescue a young man who was being held prisoner aboard a ship bound for Jamaica. The youth was heir to an estate of £800 and was being sent to be sold as a bond-servant for life in the West Indies so that another party could inherit. The bailiff, however, was refused leave to board the ship, and held at bay by armed men until the ship sailed – the fate of the young man is not known.[6]

In theory, however, after their term of indenture was over, these people would be able to resume a free life. In fact, there was sometimes little respect for law, and it would have been difficult for a bond-servant to resume their freedom if their 'owner' objected. These people, whether in America or the West Indies by their own wish or through illegal means, were at the mercy of their purchaser and the society in which they now lived. There was also the disadvantage that a convicted felon could not always return to England after his term of bondage was completed; some sentences were issued under penalty of re-imprisonment and possible execution. In Charles Dickens' novel, *Great Expectations*, Pip's benefactor, the convict Magwich, faces re-arrest and execution if he is found in England, having been sentenced to transportation for life. Even the fact that he has made a modest fortune during his time abroad does not mitigate the sentence.

As with the purchase of slaves, there was always a problem with transporting the old or sick. They might die on the trip or, worse still, not find a buyer at the other end. In August 1723 the Bristol Common Council paid 10 guineas for pardons for 7 women 'who have laine long in Newgate under sentence of transportation, and no person would take them'.[7]

Notes
1   Latimer, John, *The Annals of Bristol in the Eighteenth Century* (1970), p.188
2   Walvin, James, *Slavery and the Slave Trade: A Short Illustrated History* (1983), p.37
3   Latimer, John, op cit, p.150.
4   ibid p.152
5   ibid p.408
6   ibid p.153
7   ibid p.150

FIVE

AFRICA

The 1730s saw the zenith of the trade in African slaves with the colonies, 1739 being the year in which the greatest number of ships went out to Africa. For a few years, Bristol sent more slaving expeditions to Africa than any other city in England; however, Liverpool had replaced Bristol as the foremost trader in African slaves by 1746.

It was, of course, the Portuguese who had made the first contacts and bought the first African slaves for the Americas in the 15th century. At first they tried to raid for slaves. This proved singularly unsuccessful as they could only capture a few, and when they returned they found a large band of well-organised, well-armed tribesmen waiting for them. They therefore turned to barter with the local chieftains, who were already selling their prisoners of war to Arab traders for re-sale in the Middle East. They created a physical presence to aid this, once the trade was on a permanent and regular basis. In 1466 a Portuguese force founded the first trading fort at Sao Jorge da Mina (Elmina in Ghana), followed in 1482 by first contact with the Kingdom of Kongo. In 1493 they were settled on Sao Tomé Island in the Gulf of Guinea, and in 1505 they built a fort at Sofala on the coast of Mozambique.[1]

The most prolific producer of slaves was the area covered by Gabon, the Congo and Angola in Central Africa. From about 1400, this area was dominated by the Kongo Empire, which was surrounded by the three smaller kingdoms of Loango, Tio and Ndongo. While the Kongo Empire favoured trade with Portugal, Loango preferred to deal with England and Holland. The second largest supplier was the area centred on the Niger Delta, bounded by the Bights of Benin and Biafra. The kingdoms of Benin, Dahomey and Oyo dominated this area.[2]

Like those who came after them, the Portuguese tried to set themselves up as tribal overlords, to create settlements and to found missions to convert the natives. All attempts essentially failed. The climate was the major obstacle to permanent European settlement, with malaria and yellow fever as the biggest killers. Added to this, the people already had advanced social systems, and while they were happy to use the Europeans as traders, they were unwilling to allow them any permanent place in their society. Most of the states had a standing army, with a variety of weapons, and they were prepared to use them if need be. The only successful Portuguese entrepreneurs were those with European fathers and African mothers; some did succeed in setting up their own trading stations with 'troops' and followers.

One of the principal elements for Portuguese success was that they not only traded European goods, they also traded goods between African tribes and states. It was not so much that they introduced 'exotic' goods, as that they dramatically improved existing trade. Things that had once occasionally arrived through sporadic trade now came in larger amounts and far more frequently. The influence that they exerted was so strong that a Portuguese-based *patois* developed in many states to facilitate use of this new trade network. Slaves were only part of the Portuguese requirement in Africa. Before 1600 only about 25% of all African slaves were crossing the Atlantic; the rest were still following the route north, into the markets of the Middle East and Europe. During the 17th century, slaves still tended to come second behind such cargoes as gold, ivory, timber, hides, pepper, beeswax and gum.[3]

By the mid-1600s, the Dutch West Indies Company followed the Portuguese into the African trade and overtook them as the dominant trading power on the Slave Coast. From the 1650s onwards, the English began to make their presence felt. In the first half of the 18th Century English ships collected some two-thirds of their slaves from the Gold Coast, the Bight of Biafra and Angola; the other third came from Senegambia, the Bight of Benin and Sierra Leone.[4] Between 1672 and 1713, it is estimated that the Royal Africa Company alone transported in excess of 350,000 slaves to the West Indies.[5] However, throughout the 1600s, the Spanish, Portuguese, French, Dutch and English found themselves in competition with ships from Denmark, Sweden and Germany. The local rulers occasionally used this obvious rivalry to raise their prices and sell to the highest bidder.[6]

Not all African tribes agreed willingly to sell their captives, and their own people, to the Europeans. The kings of Benin were one dynasty of rulers who refused to become embroiled in this trade, although there is evidence that some of their followers were not so scrupulous. The question is whether the chiefs could have traded slaves unless they had tacit royal approval.

The kingdom of Dahomey tried to resist; King Agaja II (1708-1732) formed an army of his young men and women to protect his people and fight off the traders. He also sent a message (which went unanswered) to the King of England suggesting that the plantations be relocated to Africa from America and the West Indies, thereby removing the need for the Middle Passage. Unfortunately, a neighbouring tribe, the Oyo, was larger and stronger than Dahomey, and was involved in the slave trade; they resented the Dahomean stand, and needed Dahomey captives to trade. In order to protect themselves from their aggressive neighbours, the Dahomean army had to have guns; these could only come from European traders, and they would exchange them only for slaves. Dahomey, therefore, had to join the slave trading kingdoms in self defence, which they reluctantly did. Once they were in, however, they were able to use their strength to defeat the armies of Allada and Whydah, and take control of their trade, including slaving.[7]

Bristol hard-paste porcelain figure of 'Africa', c.1770. (Bristol's Museums, Galleries &
Archives)

The mechanism of local wars was graphically described in the Mercury newspaper, published in Newport, Rhode Island in July 1765. It carried an article by an English ship's captain who reported how he had heard that an Ashanti army of 50-60,000 had attacked a force of Akims and their allies, who were beaten and retreated into Fanti country. During the months of May and June, the running battles continued, until the Akim eventually surrendered. The Ashanti were therefore able to claim from 15-20,000 prisoners-of-war for slaves. Meanwhile, the Fanti, seeing the Akim out-numbered and about to be defeated, also turned on them, and invaded their lands. Thanks to the war, the Akim homeland was devastated and in a state bordering on famine. The Captain reported that he had heard that Akim civilians were giving themselves as slaves to anyone who would feed them. In a final twist, the Ashanti, once they had conquered and despoiled the Akim, turned on the Fanti. Here, however, they met their match; the Fanti were victorious and were able to capture 1,000 Ashanti to sell as slaves in their turn.[8]

Guns were only one of the trade products sold to the Africans after the Europeans had created a demand for them. In 1752 correspondence between Dr. Tucker and Lord Townsend highlighted the merchants having given spirits to the Negroes, particularly gin, in order to create a desire in them to trade for more. This market for liquor had its limits, however, as recorded by Captain John Cahoone, of Rhode Island, who wrote from Anamabo in October 1736:

> 'Sir, after my respects to you: these may inform how it is with me at present. I bless God I enjoy my health very well as yet: but am likely to have a long and troublesome voyage of it, for there never was so much rum on the coast at one time before, nor the like of the French ships never seen before for number for the whole coast is full of them. For my part I can give no guess when I shall get way, for I purchased but 27 slaves since I have been here, for slaves is very scarce. We have had nineteen sail of us at one time in the Road; so that these ships that are said to carry prime slaves off is now forced to take any that comes. Here is 7 sail of us Rum men that we are ready to devour one another; for our case is desperate.' [9]

From the moment of their purchase or capture, Africans were treated as a commodity. Slaves captured or purchased inland could be used as porters for goods also being brought to the coast for sale, the most frequent being ivory. Thus not only could a profit be realised from the sale of the slave, but their services were free and their load could also be sold. Francis Moore, a European factor to the Royal Africa Company from 1730 to 1735, sent a report to London:

> 'The [African] Merchants bring down Elephants Teeth and in some Years Slaves to the Amount of 2,000, most of which they say are Prisoners taken in War; They buy them from the different Princes who take them …

Their Way of bringing them is, tying them by the Neck with Leather-Thongs, at about a Yard distance from each other, 30 or 40 in a String, having generally a Bundle or Corn, or an Elephant's Tooth upon each of their Heads … Since this Slave-Trade has been used, all Punishments are changed into Slavery; there being an Advantage on such Condemnations, they strain for Crimes very hard, in order to get the Benefit of selling the Criminal. Not only Murder, Theft and Adultery, are punished by selling the Criminal for a Slave, but every trifling Crime is punished in the same manner.' 10

There are no figures for the number of people who died during the journey to the coast, and how many died in the forts and trading post cells, waiting for a European ship to come. The abolitionist Thomas Fowell Buxton suggested that the majority of deaths of slaves, once they had been selected for sale, occurred before they left Africa, with a much smaller percentage occurring during the Middle Passage and only a fraction immediately after arrival in the Americas. Unfortunately no statistics survive to show on what he based this assumption. If this were true, given the number of deaths known to have occurred during the Middle Passage, then the overall death rate, from start to finish, would have been millions.11

Most chiefs and kings received large profits from slave trading, whether from prisoners of war from other tribes or criminals amongst their own people. Chiefs could levy a tax on the export of slaves and demand fees for permission to trade. Their officials accepted kick-backs as 'facilitation' fees, and insisted on traders hiring 'official' interpreters. The ruler could also insist that his personal slaves were purchased first, regardless of their quality, at a premium rate; failure to buy them would seriously damage the chances of any further trading. Finally, of course, the chief set the final price for slaves, which rose and fell with supply and demand. As if this were not enough, the ships had to buy their supplies of food and particularly water for the Middle Passage from the Africans at whatever price they cared to set.

Local produce bought for the Middle Passage ideally provided two meals a day for the slaves. One would consist of rice and yams (and other native foods), and the second would be of barley, corn and biscuits. Ideally these would be supplemented with meat or fish, cooked in palm oil and seasoned with Melegueta pepper from West Africa. The Bristol ship, the *Brothers*, crossing during 55 days in 1789, carried 3lb 10ozs of yams, 2ozs of flour, 3.5ozs of beans and 10ozs of biscuit per man per day, with barrels of salted beef. For crew and slaves there was lime juice and vinegar to use as a mouthwash to prevent scurvy. The local produce increased in variety when the American traders began introducing new crops. These included maize, sweet potatoes, cassava, coffee and cocoa. European ships introduced pigs and citrus fruit.12

In 1720 Tomba, Chief of the Baga, founded a remarkable resistance movement. He tried to get all the people of the Pongo area in modern Guinea to unite and drive the slave traders and their agents out but the alliance failed. The only result was that some dealers were killed and their houses burned. A local trader managed to capture 'Captain' Tomba, and sold him into slavery, but Tomba led a ship-board revolt and was only killed in the fighting after he had already dispatched three members of the crew.[13]

Some of the traders on the coast were a unique group, the sons of European fathers and African mothers. The Portuguese were the first to intermarry and use these social connections to expand their business. The local-born trader stood in a strong position between the Africans who wished to sell and the Europeans who wished to buy. They were the interpreters and the middle-men for virtually all the deals made. They became very powerful, and some became rich from the rising prices. Amongst the literature drawn up by Bristol merchants in support of a Government Bill to found the Company of Merchants Trading to Africa, is a pamphlet dated to 1750, which highlights the rise in prices that were being asked by these agents for slaves as demand grew. In 1725 the asking price had been goods to the value of £3-£4; now it was £28-£32.[14] A very few (of English, Portuguese or French extraction) even assembled bands of followers, seized territory and set up what were virtually their own short-lived principalities.

Ship's manifests rarely mention the tribe or region of origin of the slaves they carried. This information must be deduced from the areas in which the traders were working. Before 1700 the majority came from the coastal regions. An area between the Niger and Cross River Deltas, including the states of Bonny (Niger Delta), New Calabar (Niger Delta), and Calabar (Cross River Delta), contained the Igbo and Ibibio tribes, who both suffered depredation by slaving. After 1700, because of the growing demand on the depleted coastal region, men and women from further inland could now be found in the slave markets along the coast.[15]

James Grainger (1721-1767), a doctor and occasional poet, wrote a poem entitled *The Sugar Cane* in 1759 whilst he was living in Jamaica, where he was to die of West Indian Fever.[16] In it, he sang the praises of the plantation owners and their produce, advised on the kind of slave to buy and detailed some of the tribes from which slaves could be bought, and their characteristics:

> *Must thou from Afric reinforce thy gang! –*
> *Let health and youth their every sinew firm;*
> *Clear roll their ample eye; their tongue be red;*
> *Broad swell their chest; their shoulders should expand;*
> *Not prominent their belly; clean and strong*
> *Their thighs and legs, in just proportion rise.*
> *Such soon will brave the fervours of the clime;*
> *And free from ails, that kill thy Negro-train,*
> *An useful servitude will long support ...*
> *Worms lurk in all; yet, pronest they to worms,*
> *Who from Mundingo sail. When therefore such*

Thou buy'st, for sturdy and laborious they,
Straight let some learned leech strong med'cines give,
Till food and climate both familiar grow ...
One precept more, it much imports to know
The Blacks, who drink the Quanza's lucid stream,
Fed by ten thousand streams, are prone to bloat,
Whether at home or in these ocean isles;
And though nice art the water may subdue,
Yet many die; and few, for many a year,
Just strength attain to labour for their lord.
Wouldst thou secure thine Ethiop from these ails,
Which change of climate, change of waters breed,
And food unusual? Let Machon draw
From each some blood, as age and sex required.

Another description of the preferred origin of slaves comes from a letter from Benjamin King and Robert Arbuthnot, slave agents in Antigua, to Isaac Hobhouse and Stephen Baugh in Bristol. In a letter dated 24th November 1740, the agents wrote to their principals:

> *'We would you could be persuaded to direct your vessels to the Gold Coast or Widdaw, as Negroes from those places, especially the latter, are in most esteem here and will always sell at good prices, when Bonny Negroes (the men particularly) are held in much contempt, comparatively with the others, and indeed, such numbers being imported, and many of them hanging and drowning themselves, has taken many people from purchasing them, tho' it must be allowed that the boys, girls, and women prove good slaves, but the men are wretched bad and scarce of any value, as one of us has sufficiently experienced and would not bring them into his Estate on any consideration.'* [17]

Yet another source of information on the origin of the slaves may be found in West Indian work songs, like this one:

If me want to go in a Ebo,
Me can't go there!
Since dem tief [thief] me from a Guinea,
Me can't go there!
If me want for go in a Kongo,
Me can't go there!
Since dem tief me from my tatta [home],
Me can't go there![18]

The ships waiting to load slaves ran a strong risk of crew illness and death from the tropical diseases rife on the coast. In August 1767, an agent in Old Calabar wrote to his company in Liverpool that there were presently seven vessels in the harbour, each hoping to load about 500 slaves. Unfortunately for them, there were hardly any to be had: 'the natives are at variance with each other'. He went on to report that 'the river of late has been very fatal'; he listed three captains of Bristol ships dead of disease, and a large number of crewmen, and added pessimistically, 'I do not expect that our stay here will exceed eight months'.[19]

One element of the problem was that as the demand for slaves increased, the coastal populations had either been enslaved already, were unsuitable, indispensable or had fled; the slavers had to go further inland to purchase, capture and kidnap the Africans they needed. The ships might, therefore, have to wait longer periods in order to load up with slaves, unless they had an agent working for them, assembling a cargo in advance of their arrival. As early as March 1729, the Jamaican agents, Tyndall & Assheton, were writing to Isaac Hobhouse warning him of the problems of taking too many people; the trade on the Bight of Biafra 'must be overdone, as we fear a Little time will discover'.[20]

The danger was not just from infection and disease. There were several instances of slaves rebelling. An early example was in 1721; the *Robert* of Bristol (Agents, Richard Arding & Co.; Master, Richard Arding) was loading 160 slaves on the Ivory Coast when a revolt occurred. Three of the crew were killed before the revolt was brought under control, and three of the slaves were executed as an example.[21]

In February 1753, the *Marlborough* had finished loading about 400 slaves at Bonny. The crew was short-handed, so 28 slaves were selected to help man the ship. Three days out, the 28 managed to get hold of weapons and whilst the sailors were cleaning out the holds, they attacked and killed the captain and the deck watch. In all, 35 crewmen were killed, although seven were spared to help sail the ship back to Bonny. Another slaving vessel, the *Hawk* out of Bristol, tried to retake the *Marlborough*, but they were beaten off by the Negroes, who had a good supply of guns and knew how to use them. It turned out that about 270 of the slaves were from Bonny, and a substantial number of the rest from the Gold Coast. There was an argument as to where they should land, and a fight broke out, ending in the deaths of some 100 of the Africans. In the event, the ship was halted and the Bonny survivors landed; the remaining 150 Gold Coast Negroes, with the 6 surviving English sailors, sailed off, and were never seen or heard of again.[22]

Another hazard came from European and Eastern ships – pirates and privateers. Pirates were always active, with the added danger of privateers during times of war. In 1719, the *Peterborough* (Agents, John Duckinfield & Co.; Master, John Owen) was captured off the African coast by pirates, and fitted out to serve as a pirate vessel. In the same year pirate Captain Edward England of the *Royal James* seized the *Bentworth* out of Bristol, despite her crew of 30 and 12 guns.[23]

The firm of John Duckinfield & Co. was unlucky again in November 1720, when

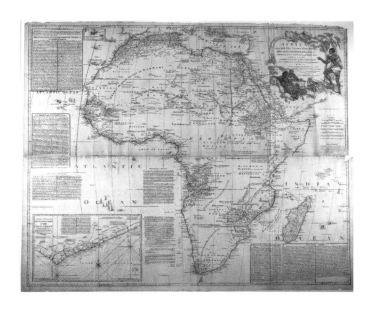

The north-western African coast was the source of most of Britain's slave trading. Africa, with all its States, Kingdoms, Republics, Regions, Islands, etc, 1794, based on d'Anville's map…by S Boulton [detail] University of Bristol Specialist Library, catalogue no. 53.

the Governor of Virginia seized their ship, the *Prince Eugene*. Her master, Captain Stratton, was charged with having illegal East India goods in his cargo, which had come from Madagascar (including 103 slaves) – the charges concluded that he had been dealing with the pirates who used the island as a base in the Indian Ocean. Morgan Miles, one of the crew, reported that as the ship approached Yorktown, they moored in Chesapeake Bay, and the captain ordered the unloading of six bags and six chests of silver coins, which were then buried. Miles said the coins were the result of the captain trading with the pirate Captain Condell of the *Dragon* for brandy and other cargo to the value of £9,000 in Spanish silver dollars. He had also used his contacts with the pirates to buy slaves at a lower price than he would have paid on the Guinea Coast.[24]

Pirates were a double problem, since they were active both off the African coast and in West Indian waters. In the early 1700s the pirate stronghold in the Caribbean was on Providence Island in the Bahamas. A rough survey of the origins of those pirates who could be interviewed after they were arrested or pardoned, suggests that about 35% were English, 10% Scottish and 8% Welsh. The rest were a mixture of American (25%), West Indian (20%, from Jamaica, Barbados and the Bahamas), and the remainder from Sweden, Holland, France, Spain and Portugal. Most of the English pirates claimed London as their home, although quite a few were from the West Country and some from Bristol.[25]

In 1724 Captain Roger Stevens of Bristol, on his way to Jamaica, had his ship attacked and burnt after it had been looted. He and his bos'n were marooned on the island of Rattan by the pirates.[26] Marooning was a recognised way for pirates to dispose of crews of ships they seized and to punish dissenters amongst their own men. In October 1704 the pirate Captain Stradling, master of the *Cinque Ports* (originally commanded by Captain William Dampier), marooned a member of his crew in Mas-a-Tierra, one of the Juan Fernandez Islands. It was not until February 1709 that the sailor, Alexander Selkirk, was rescued by Captain Woodes Rogers of Bristol, and brought back to England on the *Duke*. Legend has it that Selkirk stayed in Bristol and it was at the *Llandogger Trow* public house in King Street that he met the writer Daniel Defoe, who turned his story into a famous novel.[27]

Captain Woodes Rogers was to play a large part in destroying the power base of the pirates in the Caribbean. In the 17th century the governors of Jamaica had actually encouraged the pirates to use Port Royal as a base. The presence of so many armed pirate ships discouraged French or Spanish forces from attacking the colonies and looting Port Royal itself. Added to this, the free-spending pirates boosted the local economy, particularly in the brothels and public houses (of which there were many). Since most of their loot was Spanish in origin, a blind eye could be turned. In the 1660s, the town was home to Captain Henry Morgan, and it was in Port Royal that he and his crew spent the fortune they gained from a raid on the Spanish city of Portobello.

In June 1721 Governor Phenney of New Providence reported that a Bristol ship had been attacked near Jamaica by the pirate ship *Good Fortune*. The crew was led by Captain Anstead and of the 80 crewmen, 19 were recorded as Negroes. A surprising number of pirate crewmen were black or mulatto. Some were slaves who had run away, while others were free men. From the details of pirate trials, crews could comprise as much as one-sixth Negroes. Some of the convicted black pirates were hanged with their comrades, others were sold into (or back into) slavery.

However, not all the Negroes served as full crew members. Most were kept in a state of virtual slavery by the pirates, acting as servants and doing all the heavy work on board. Some slaves were sold by the pirates after the ships on which they were being transported were captured, as the pirates were not averse to slave trading if it made them a profit. The infamous Captain Henry Morgan owned an estate on the island of Jamaica and more than 100 slaves.[28]

In the 18th century, however, it was decided that the pirates were a menace to all shipping that had to be dealt with. Pirates became unwelcome and the British government authorised privateers to hunt them down. Pirates no longer came to Port Royal to spend their loot on pleasure; the town was now a prison and it was here that many pirates were hanged. Captain Woodes Rogers was Governor of the Bahamas from 1717, and one of his major responsibilities was the eradication of piracy. He was largely successful, but ill-health forced him to return to England for a time, and eventually cut short his life.[29] Apart from pirates, another danger was privateers. In times of war, every government authorised nationalist 'pirates' who were licensed to prey only on enemy shipping. In 1709 the *Joseph and Thomas* of Bristol was seized by a French privateer, le Briliant; in January 1710 the ship, under French control, was loading slaves on Cape Coast. It left Whydah for the French West Indies with a cargo of slaves on 15 February but as luck would have it, was re-taken by a British privateer just off the coast of Martinique.[30] In 1741 the *Swallow* was seized by a Spanish privateer three days out of Bristol, and taken to San Sebastian. The Agents Michael Becher & Co.set the value of ship and cargo at £4,200.[31]

What with the climate and disease, the Africans, the agents, the merchants, pirates and privateers of other countries, it would seem that the Bristol ships and their crews had sufficient trouble. However, in 1737 the Bristol merchants made representation to the British Admiralty to complain about three Royal Navy ships, the Diamond, the Greenwich and the Spence. These ships were supposed to be protecting the British vessels, but they were engaged in slaving on their own account. They had come out from England loaded with trade goods – including cotton stuffs, liquor and gunpowder – and were adding insult to injury by gazumping the prices offered by the legitimate traders (£30 a head for slaves, about £4 over the going rate). The *Greenwich*, they reported, had left with about 200 slaves, whilst the *Spence* had between 50 and 60.[32]

Notes
1   Klein, Herbert S, *The Atlantic Slave Trade* (1999), p.51
2   Klein, Herbert S, op cit, p.63-5
3   ibid, p.56
4   Richardson, David, Bristol, *Africa and the 18 Century Slave Trade to America: The Years of Decline* 1746-68, Vol.3 (1991), p.xix
5   Klein, Herbert S, op cit, p.80
6   ibid, p.77
7   ibid, p.117
8   Plimmer, Charlotte & Denis, *Slavery, The Anglo-American Involvement* (1973), p.52
9   Plimmer, Charlotte & Denis, op cit, p.44
10   ibid, p.42
11   Klein, Herbert S, op cit, p.128
12   ibid, p.94]
13   Sherwood, Marika, *Black Peoples in the Americas* (1992), p.28
14   Latimer, John, op cit, p.271
15   Klein, Herbert S, op cit, p.115
16   DB Wyndham Lewis & Charles Lee (eds), *The Stuffed Owl: An Anthology of Bad Verse* (1963), p.90-1
17   MacInnes, C.M., A Gateway of Empire (1968), p.207
18   Brathwaite, Edward Kamau, *Folk Culture of the Slaves in Jamaica* (1971), p.20
19   Latimer, John, op cit, p.380
20   Richardson, David (ed.), op cit, p.xxii
21   ibid p.98
22   Latimer, John, op cit, p.301
23   Cordingly, David, *Life among the Pirates, The Romance and Reality* (1995), p.131
24   Cordingly, David, op cit, p.208-9
25   ibid p.26
26   ibid p.161
27   ibid p.165
28   ibid p.27
29   ibid p.178
30   Richardson, David (ed.) op cit, p.17
31   ibid p.122
32   Latimer, John, *The History of the Society of Merchant Venturers of the City of Bristol* (1903), p.181

SIX

THE MIDDLE PASSAGE

One of the most complete accounts and one of the few contemporary records by a slave, is the *Interesting Narrative of the Life of Olaudah Equiano*, published in 1789 in London. Equiano had been kidnapped in 1756, aged 11. He wrote in graphic detail about the horrors of the Middle Passage:

> *'I was soon put down under the decks [where] with the loathsomeness of the stench and my grief I became so sick and low that I was not able to eat ... For refusing to eat, I was flogged ... I would have jumped over the side [of the ship] but I could not... The crew used to watch us very closely who were not chained down to the decks... Amongst the poor chained men I found some of my own nation which in a small degree gave ease to my mind.'*
>
> *'The stench of the hold now that the whole ship's cargo was confined together became absolutely pestilential. The closeness of the place and the heat and the crowding, which meant that each had scarcely room to turn himself, almost suffocated us.'* Equiano described, *'sickness among the slaves, of which many died... The situation was aggravated by the galling of the chains and the filth of the necessary tubs ... The shrieks of the women and the groans of the dying rendered the whole a scene of horror almost inconceivable.'*

The problem here was that if the ship were delayed by bad weather, not only would the time spent in the hold be longer, but also there would be few opportunities to allow the slaves on deck, or to clean out the holds where they were imprisoned. Even those who died could be left shackled to those still living (normally, dead slaves would be thrown overboard as soon as they were discovered). The biggest killer was dysentery, almost inevitable in cramped conditions where food and water would almost certainly become polluted. The effects of such illness are graphically described in the journal of Captain William Miller, master of the *Black Prince* which sailed from the Gold Coast on 1 March 1763, bound for Antigua with 488 slaves on board:

> *'3 March...Slaves is very indifferent with Colds and Purging*

[vomiting]…Woman No.11 died. 8 March…One Woman is very bad, Many of them with purging and some falls away [loose weight] not eating… 14 March…The slaves fore and aft [in both holds] falls away very much although no visible complaint, eat their victuals very well… 1 April…The slaves still fall away and complain of gripings [cramps] and fluxes [diarrhoea, sometimes bloody]… 10 April Slaves is much worse and this dirty weather can't get them up [on deck] tho fall away…19 April…The Slaves still complaining of griping and falls away as it have not been in our power to keep them up half a day this month past…29 April…Washed all the Slaves fore and aft the first time since we left the coast…' [1]

Equiano went on to describe how, because he was a child, he was allowed on deck when he got sick. On one occasion, some of the slaves came up on deck for air and exercise; 'when we had a smooth wind and moderate sea, two of my wearied countrymen who were chained together, preferring death to such a life of misery, somehow made through the nettings and jumped into the sea.'[2] The netting was fixed so as to prevent this kind of thing. A letter of instruction from Isaac Hobhouse & Co. to one of their masters reads, 'So soon as you begin to slave, let the netting be fixed breast high fore and aft, and so keep them shackled and hand-bolted, to prevent their rising or leaping overboard.[3]

The loss of life continued as the ships left the African coast, not just as a result of illness. In 1762, the *Defence* of Bristol was sunk off the coast of Callebar; the crew was saved, but the cargo of 460 slaves were all drowned.[4]

One of the worst aspects of the Middle Passage, however, remained the mortality rate due to sickness. The *Greyhound* (Agents, Isaac Hobhouse & Co.; Master, Edward Halden) carried 189 men, 128 women, 16 boys and six girls on a passage in 1722 – of these 339 people, 130 died during the 50-day voyage to Barbados. About 30 of the survivors were sold in Barbados, the rest being sent on to Virginia. In the same year, the *Joseph and Anne* (Agents, Abraham Hooke & Co.) reported that they had 'buried' 70 out of a cargo of 309 slaves on the way from Africa to Montserrat.[5] The *Mary* (Agent, Richard Farr & Co.; Master Robert Bibbee) sailed in 1731 from Bristol to Bonny, then to St. Kitts and Jamaica; on January 2, Captain Bibbee reported that he was carrying 260 slaves, but that sickness had already claimed his carpenter and 6 seamen. From Bonny ('that unwholesome place'), he went on to have a 'very sickly Voyage', eventually losing 20 out of 27 crew and 141 slaves. Captain Bibbee was listed as being part-owner of the 21 cwt. of ivory that formed part of the return cargo, but it did him little good as he died shortly after returning to Bristol.[6] In 1764 the *St. Michael* of Bristol arrived at St. Kitts, having lost to illness 200 slaves, the captain, chief mate and 11 crewmen.[7]

A fascinating book, *The Life and Adventures of Silas Todd*, purported to be an account of the voyages of a young sailor. In 1727 he had served on board a slaving ship, under

From the moment of their purchase or capture, Africans were treated as a commodity. 'The Frigate Southwell trading on ye coast of Africa', detail, print by Nicholas Pococke, c.1760. (Bristol's Museums, Galleries & Archives)

Captain Tucker (possibly Captain Timothy Tucker). The account of the voyage includes a description of another hazard of the Middle Passage; at about midnight the slaves grew excited, claiming that 'Egbo', whom Todd identified as the Devil, was loose on board. By morning 41 out of the 80 slaves were dead, apparently from fright. Todd also reported that the captain took against the free Negro cook, and subjected him to a series of beatings and scarrings, until the cook committed suicide.[8]

Even for those who survived the Middle Passage, the dangers were not over. The Caribbean and Gulf of Mexico were very liable to hurricanes. In 1712 a hurricane hit Jamaica; it destroyed 38 ships at anchor in Port Royal and nine at Kingston. The galley *Dursley* was wrecked on Morant Keys, Jamaica in 1725, with loss of cargo and the death by drowning of 40 Negroes.[9] A hurricane sank the *Triton* (Agent, Henry Tonge & Co.; Master, Thomas Robbins) in October 1743. She was laden with 336 slaves from the Gold Coast and Anamaboe, some of whom had already been sold at Barbados before the ship met the storm.[10] The *Prince of Orange* (Agent, Richard Farr & Co.; Master Japhet Bird) arrived in St. Kitts in 1736. As she neared port, 100 of the 273 slaves on board jumped over the side and 33 were drowned. 'More of them were taken up almost drown'd, some of them died since, but not to the Owners' Loss, they being sold before any Discovery was made of the Injury the Salt water had done them'.[11]

The Middle Passage carried so many dangers to the health and life of the men serving on board that it became more and more difficult to find crews. The men knew that the voyage would be long, that they would be subject to possible infectious disease, both whilst waiting to load in African ports and on the Middle Passage. The sailors summed up their fears in the well-known verse:

Beware and take care of the Bight of Benin
For one that comes out, there are forty go in.

The crews also had to face the severity of the captains who sailed on the Triangular Trade. Men like John Newton might serve as master of a slaving ship whilst studying for Holy Orders, but there is also the record of masters like Captain John Jayne of Bristol, who was hung on the Thames Bank in May 1726. He had been sentenced to death for 'the atrocious murder of his cabin boy at sea'. A similar captain was Commander Rice Harris, a Bristol slaver hung in June 1733 for murdering one of his crew 'in circumstances of horrible barbarity.'[12] In 1735 Captain James Newton was sentenced to hang for murdering his wife; rather than face his execution, he took poison while in prison. Newton had previously been tried for piracy, but not convicted, and was known to have killed at least four of his crewmen. It was little wonder that sailors preferred almost any ship to a slaver.[13]

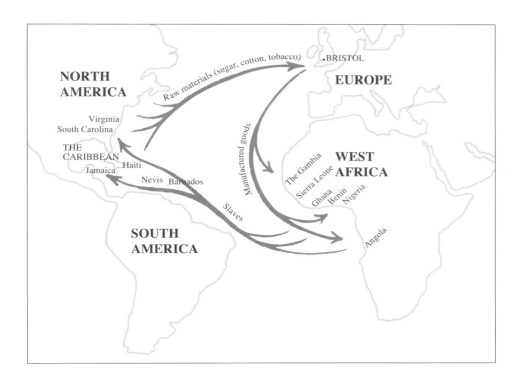

FIVE

Ships left Bristol for Africa and took the slaves from there to the West Indies and North America before returning to Bristol with trade goods; this was known as the Triangular Trade. Map showing the 'triangle' of the Transatlantic Slave Trade.
(Bristol's Museums, Galleries & Archives)

Notes
1   Dresser, Madge & Giles, Sue, Bristol and Transatlantic Slavery (2000), p.126
2   Oladaudah Equiano, The Interesting Narrative of the Life of Olaudah Equiano (1995)
3   Robinson, Derek, *A Shocking History of Bristol* (1973), p.60
4   Latimer, John, *The Annals of Bristol in the Eighteenth Century* (1970), p.343
5   Richardson, David (ed.) *Bristol, Africa and the 18th Century Slave Trade to America: Years of Expansion 1698-1729*, Vol.1 (1986), p.102-3
6   Richardson, David (ed.), op cit, p.23
7   Latimer, John, op cit, p.343
8   John Taylor, *A Book About Bristol* (1872), p.328-9
9   Richardson, David (ed.), op cit, p.133
10   ibid p.139
11   ibid p.75
12   Latimer, John, op cit, p.151
13   ibid 192 -3

SEVEN

WEST INDIES & NORTH AMERICA

Between 1730 and 1745 the destination of the Bristol slave ships tended to be limited to the West Indies and North America. Of the recorded voyages, 245 cargoes of slaves went direct to Jamaica, 61 to St. Kitts, 34 to Barbados, 11 to Antigua, and two each to Montserrat and Nevis; 65 to Virginia, 56 to South Carolina, and eight to Maryland. One reason for the prominent number of ships going to Jamaica was that it was from this island that the vessels supplying slaves to the Spanish Indies set out. This, of course, was the trade made legal by the Assiento Clause – between 1715 and 1738, 231 ships carrying slaves were recorded out of Jamaica to Spanish territories.[1]

The numbers of slaves in the West Indies increased enormously during the middle years of the 18th century. In 1700 there were around 45,000 African slaves in Jamaica; by 1780, there were nearly 200,000. In French controlled St. Domingue, the increase was even more dramatic – from about 16,000 in 1700 to around 500,000 in 1750.[2]

The ratio of black to white was hardly astonishing – in Barbados in 1713 there were 45,000 slaves and 16,000 white adults; in Jamaica in the same year there were 55,000 slaves and only 7,000 whites.[3] The large numbers of African slaves and the low number of white owners explains, in part, the savage cruelty with which the slaves were used. It was felt that the slaves would revolt and murder the hopelessly out-numbered owners unless the slightest infringement was met with savage retribution. Hence striking a white man was punishable by death, stealing was dealt with by flogging and mutilation, unsuccessfully running away was countered with beatings, mutilations and being forced to work loaded in chains. There was also the threat that the slave would be sold on, leaving behind friends and family – a female slave who offended could be separated from her partner and her children, or see her offspring sold away from her.

Olaudah Equiano left a description of the landing and selling of slaves in Barbados:

> *'At last we anchored off Bridgetown. Many merchants and planters now came on board. They put us in separate parcels and examined us attentively. They also made us jump... Soon after we were landed there came to us Africans of all languages. We were conducted immediately to*

*the merchant's yard, where we were pent up together like so many sheep ...
We were not many days in the merchant's custody before we were sold ...
On a signal given, with much noise and clamour, the buyers rushed into
the yard where we were confined, and made choice of that parcel they like
best ... In this manner, without scruple, are relations and friends separated,
most of them never to see each other again.'[4]*

Owners, on the other hand, passed laws reflecting their superiority within the law.
In Bermuda in 1730 a law was passed that stated that a European could not be fined
or executed for killing a slave or a Negro. A further law that year made it a criminal
offence for a free African to remain in Bermuda for longer than 6 months after they
had been freed, in case they gave the slaves aspirations or made them discontented.[5]

The colonies were not happy to be simply used as a source of raw materials by a
demanding homeland. From 1724 onwards, the West Indian colonies tried to set a
potentially very lucrative tax on imported slaves. As can be imagined, Bristol was one
of the strongest lobbyists against such a law, although the colonies did eventually get
their own way and set such a tax. In 1742 South Carolina set enormous import duties
on slaves. By 1775 Bristol's M.P. Edmund Burke wrote that Jamaica had imposed 'a
very great duty on all Negroes over 30 years of age brought in'.[6] In 1774 the
Jamaican Legislature wanted to pass a law limiting the number of slaves imported
each year. The Bristol merchants, along with representatives from Liverpool, opposed
the measure; 'We cannot allow the colonists to check or discourage in any degree a
traffic so beneficial to the nation.'[7]

Once a slave had arrived in the West Indies, it was illegal for anyone to help them
leave the islands whilst they were still in the condition of slavery. However, a
remarkable story unfolded in 1767 – the two sons of the King of Old Town, Old
Calabar, were taken prisoner in a local skirmish and sold as slaves. They were
transported to the West Indies, where they escaped the islands and headed for
Virginia. Here they were able to find a ship that would sign them on as crew, sailing
to Bristol. On arrival, they contacted a merchant called Jones, who had had dealings
with their father. He 'got them taken off the ship with a writ of Habeas Corpus', and
sent them back to Old Calabar in one of his ships. Merchant Jones thereby obtained
the undying gratitude of the King of Calabar, no bad thing in this period of high
competition for slaves.[8]

Not all slaves could seek their freedom as these young men did. Some of those in
the West Indies ran away from the plantations and joined the Maroons (or
Cimaroons) who lived in the hills and mountains. They were the descendants of early
runaway slaves and the native inhabitants. Those who stayed as slaves could resist
their captivity by working as slowly and as badly as they could, and by refusing to
completely surrender their African identity.

Notes

1 Richardson, David (ed.) *Bristol, Africa and the 18th Century Slave Trade to America: Years of Ascendancy 1730-1745*, Vol.2 (1987), p.xviii, xx

2 Walvin, James, *Slavery and the Slave Trade* (1983), p.35-6

3 Walvin, James, op cit, p.111

4 Olaudah Equiano, (ed Robert J Allison), *The Interesting Narrative of the Life of Olaudah Equiano* (1995)

5 Craton, Michael, Walvin, James & Wright, *David, Slavery, Abolition and Emancipation* (1976), p.179-80

6 Latimer, John, *The History of the Society of Merchant Venturers of the City of Bristol* (1903), p.184

7 Latimer, John, *The Annals of Bristol in the Eighteenth Century* (1970), p.413

8 Pope-Hennessy, James, *Sins of the Fathers* (1967), p.202

EIGHT

BRISTOL

In 1739 war was declared with Spain and by 1744, France entered the conflict. The Bristol Corporation sent a petition to the King complaining of the 'depredations and cruelties' of the Spanish and asking for protection for the African trade ships, given that French and other foreign privateers were said to infest the Bristol Channel and beyond. Their depredations were driving insurance costs prohibitively high and drastically reduced the number of ships sailing for Africa, America and the West Indies. On a more practical level, 90 merchants pledged £100 each to fit and arm cruisers to protect the ships on the voyages. While Liverpool fitted out three ships, the vessels produced by Bristol were:

Southwell	*400 tons*	*24 guns*	*200 men*
Bristol	*550 tons*	*38 guns*	*300 men*
Leviathon		*28 guns*	*250 men*
Rover		*24 guns*	*210 men*
Townsend		*22 guns*	*180 men*

In her first 4 months of service, the *Southwell* took 8 prizes, and the privateers proved to be highly profitable to owners and sailors – these ships, at least, never had any trouble finding a crew. Not only did they stand to make a lot of money, but they were also exempt from the notorious Royal Navy Press Gang. The *Queen of Hungary*, out of Bristol, took a prize with a cargo valued at £20,000,[1] which provided an incentive to the crew, who often received a share of the prize money rather than a fixed wage. *The Gloucester Journal* of 4 September 1744 recorded:

> *'Nothing is to be seen here [in Bristol] but rejoicing for the great number of French prizes brought in. Our sailors are in the highest spirits, full of money, and spend their whole time in carousing ... dressed out with Laced Hats, Tassels, Swords with Sword Knots, and in short all things that can give them an opportunity to spend their money.'*

The Press Gang, recruiting crews for the Royal Navy, were a real threat to the citizens of Bristol and to sailors in general. In September 1756 the *Virginia Merchant*, coming in from the West Indies, was anchored at Kingroad when the Press Gang appeared and threatened to seize the crew. These men had just completed an arduous year's voyage, and so resisted forcefully. A naval tender was called in and fired on the ship, killing and wounding members of the crew, and the ship was sunk where she lay.[2] No one in Bristol was safe. In July 1779, the Press Gang were on the prowl and seized a middle-aged man who had the look of a sailor. Sadly the gentleman was Mr James Caton, a retired ship's captain, but now a ship owner and merchant. The abduction actually took place in the Corn Exchange, and a magistrate's order was immediately sent to the officers of the Press Gang ordering his release. The order was ignored and a writ of habeus corpus was obtained while Burke, the city's MP, contacted the Admiralty. Unlike the humbler detainees, Mr Caton was released and successfully sued the officers of the Press Gang for £150.[3]

In 1747 (and again in 1748 and 1749) the London-based merchants made a last attempt to regain control of the Africa Trade. They claimed that more forts were needed to protect the trade in general, and that it needed a single (monopoly) company to finance this, and therefore run it. Bristol again leapt to the defence of a free trade:

> '...the principal and most considerable branch belonging to the city, and that since such trade has been free and open it has greatly increased, and His Majesty's plantations thereby much better supplied with Negroes, and larger quantities of the manufactures of this kingdom exported.'[4]

Since there was something to be said for maintaining the forts, in 1750 Bristol supported a Bill for an open and joint company to maintain them on the African coast. Bristol, Liverpool and London should each send three representatives to sit on a committee who would administer the forts and trading stations and Parliament should pay for their upkeep.[5] Bristol spent about £1,000 lobbying for this Bill to be passed and was refunded half this amount by the newly-founded Company of Merchants Trading to Africa. The Act setting up the company recorded:

> 'Whereas the Trade to and from Africa is very advantageous to Great Britain, and necessary for the supplying of the Plantations and Colonies thereunto belonging with a sufficient Number of Negroes at reasonable Rates; and for that Purpose the said Trade ought to be free and open to all his Majesty's Subjects: Therefore be it enacted, and it is hereby enacted by the King's most Excellent Majesty, by and with the Advice and Consent of the Lords Spiritual and Temporal, and Commons, in this present Parliament assembled, and by the Authority of the same, That It shall and may be lawful for all his Majesty's Subjects to trade and traffick to and from any Port or Place in Africa, between the Port of Sallee in South Barbary, and the Cape of Good Hope, when, and at such Times, and in

such Manner, and in or with such Quantity of Goods, Wares or
Merchandises, as he or they shall think fit.[6]

In fact, it was open to any merchant who could pay the £2 admission fee. In 1755, according to a local list, Bristol had 237 registered members, London had 147 and Liverpool had 89.[7]

At the height of the slave trade during the 1730s some 20 merchants dominated the business. The same names occur again and again, in all aspects of the Africa Trade. In 1729 a ship called the *Susanna* was trading on the Guinea coast; amongst her owners were Thomas and Phillip Freke; the agents for at least one voyage were William Freke & Co., and the company that provided some of the outset cargo was Thomas Freke & Co.[8] The *Oldbury*, sailing in 1720, had Richard Henvill & Co. as agents, whilst one of the factors at Montserrat was Robert Henvill, and in the same year, the *Morning Star's* agents were Joseph Jefferis & Co. and two of the several owners were John and Richard Jefferis.[9]

Possibly Bristol's most prolific slave trader was James Laroche. Between 1728 and 1769 his name was associated with 132 slaving voyages; from 1698 to 1807 no other merchant seems to have come close to this tally. Laroche originally came from London where he was apprenticed to a Guinea merchant (a slave trader);[10] young James became the man's agent about a year after he completed his apprenticeship. According to his indenture, his father was a 'gentleman', and our James may be one and the same as the famous child soprano, little Jemmie Laroche, who delighted the London theatre-goers. His career, however, lay in Bristol and in trade. The voyage of the privateer *Southwell* in 1747 indicated that the owners of the vessel were Michael Miller, Thomas Deane, W Alleyn, Cranfield Becher and James Laroche. By 1747 he was MP for Bodmyn and used his seat in Parliament to support Bristol and its stand for free trade in slaves; in 1772 the Bristol Council sent gifts of wine to their two sitting MP's and to 'Mr James Laroche, one of the Common Council and MP for Bodmyn...for his services in Parliament'. He received the gift until 1779, then it ceased; 'owing to commercial misfortunes, Sir James then retired from Parliament'.[11]

On 1 June 1759 Laroche's name appears amongst the members of the Company of Merchants Trading to Africa.[12] Some time around 1762 William Coker, a West Indies agent, wrote to John Pinney:

> *'Mr Oliver...advised me by all means to ship to Bristol...and*
> *assured me that Mr Laroche was a Gentleman of much Consequence.*
> *Upon this, I engaged 15 casks on the 'Britania' [in 1734 William Oliver*
> *was Captain of the Levant frigate owned by James Laroche & Co], which*
> *were all he could take and consigned them to the above Gentleman.'*

Pinny went on to deal with Laroche, so much so that when he was considering giving some of his business to William Reeves, he wrote that he felt, 'Laroche has behaved to me in every respect genteel and becoming the gentleman' and that he therefore felt bad about reducing their business.[13]

Laroche was one of those prominent citizens who supported King George III in his bid to crush the rebellious Americans; in return, he received a peerage. Sir James Laroche Baronet had already purchased the house and estate of Over at Almondsbury, just outside Bristol; he was living there in 1775 when his name appears in *Sketchley's Directory of Bristol*. In 1789 the elderly Sir James attended a pro-slavery meeting held at Merchants' Hall, hosted by Bristol merchants and owners of estates in the West Indies.

The 'aristocracy' of Bristol was based not on birth, but on wealth – the merchants were the leaders of society. Andrew Hooke, a Bristol publisher, said of the city, 'if we indulge a free Enquiry into the true Source and Origin of Honour, we shall find that Commerce is the sole foundation, and Solid Basis that supports not only secondary Dignities, but even Royalty itself.'[14]

The city enjoyed a riot of building in the 18th century, when the riches of the merchants and Corporation were channelled into bricks and stone to show off their prosperity. Between 1701 and 1704 a new Council House was built between Corn Street and Broad Street in the heart of the mercantile centre of the old city. It cost the grand sum of £1,146 14s 0d; it had a common hall (used as a courtroom, etc.) and offices on the ground floor, with the Council Chamber on the first floor.[15] In 1717 a Committee of the Mayor and members of the Corporation proposed building 'a more convenient Place than the Tolzey for the assembling of Merchants'. In 1722, Parliament passed an Act authorising the building of the Exchange, but local politics intervened;[16] it was 1740 before the foundation stone was laid and 1743 before the Exchange opened for business. Two years later, the Markets, behind the Exchange, opened for trade – the Open Market can be visited today.[17]

If commercial construction flourished, so too did the arts and culture. In 1735 Cranfield Becher (a slave trader), John Heylyn (related to Edmund Heylyn, a slave trader), Morgan Smith and William Barnes Jnr., all wealthy merchants, gave four tenements in Prince Street to be demolished and the site used for an Assembly Rooms. The land was donated to the Council, who leased it back to the four men for a payment of £400 and an annual rent of £5, providing they built and operated the Rooms as agreed, and with the proviso that they could keep the profits. Here, then, was the city's first custom-built social centre; the Assembly Rooms functioned until 1811 when the Clifton Rooms were built, at which time the building became a theatre. It was finally demolished in 1909 by the Great Western Railway.[18]

In 1738 a new library was proposed and the old one in King Street demolished. By 1740 the new building had arisen on the site at a cost of £1,301 8s 1d, using three of Bristol's finest masons as builders – Thomas Reynolds, George Walker and James Paty.[19] The building remained a library until 1907 and is now a restaurant.

Domestic construction also increased, with the wealth of trade financing new houses, streets and crescents in the fashionable suburbs, particularly Clifton. In the early years of the 18th century, the population of Clifton comprised mostly those who worked in the limekilns, the dockyards and in various city trades. It was really from about 1712 onwards that the great houses were built, many of them for men who had made their fortunes from the slave trade or its products. Most of them were members of the Society of Merchant Venturers, a limited, tightly-knit group of some 100 members at the beginning and end of the 18th century, whose membership rose to an all-time high of 145 in 1738-40 (the zenith of the slave trade).[20]

Clifton Hill House was built by Thomas Paty for Paul Fisher, a linen draper and ship-owner, and a noted slave trader. From 1731-3 his ship *Postboy* averaged 344 slaves to each voyage and in the year of his death one of his ships, the *Scipio*, carried 300 slaves to the West Indies. His son Paul II was not directly involved in the Guinea trade – he was a partner with Slade Baker and William Griffin and they imported cambric and linen from France and Holland and rice from Carolina. He was also part-owner of three privateers that operated during the War of the Austrian Succession (1739-1748), the *Eagle*, the *Jamaica* and the *North Cape*.[21] Clifton Court was the home of the metal-founder William Champion. While he was not a slave trader his copper works at Warmley made 'Guinea manillos and Guinea rods, kettles and pans, Guinea kettles, Guinea neptunes, &c.' between 1746 and 1761 for the slave trade with Africa. His partners were Thomas Goldney, owner of Goldney House, Thomas Crosby and Sampson Lloyd, who was Champion's brother-in-law. Champion also owned a privateer, the *Nancy*, which operated during the Seven Years War (1756-63).

Richard Farr, another leading slave trader, bought Clifton Wood House from the Countess of Huntingdon; his son, Richard Farr II, also lived there. He also ran several privateers, the *Resolution, Phoenix, Anson, Gloucester, Hanover, Planter, Indian Queen* and *True Briton*; the *Marlborough* doubled as a slave trading vessel and managed to get at least one cargo of slaves to Jamaica. Farr was Master of the Merchant Venturers in 1762, Mayor in 1763, traded on the Triangular Route with 37 recorded voyages from 1747-72, and went bankrupt in 1778. His company, Richard Farr & Co., had made heavy losses during the American War of Independence so that Richard Farr II and his sons Thomas (Sheriff in 1762 and Mayor in 1775) and Paul (Master of the Merchant Venturers in 1775) were ruined together; in 1715 Thomas was owed £8,200 for colonial trade deals in South Carolina.[23]

Many of the more notable families in Clifton were connected with slave trading or privateering – Fisher, Champion, Farr, Hobhouse, Elton, Brickdale and Jones. Henry Hobhouse rented Cornwallis House in Hotwells in the mid-1700s until at least 1785; his wealth had been inherited from his uncle Isaac Hobhouse, Agent for 44 slaving voyages. In 1750 Abraham Elton (Sheriff, Mayor and Master of the Merchant Venturers), grandson of Sir Abraham of Clevedon Court and Whitestaunton Manor, bought Freemantle House for the princely sum of £500. His nephew Isaac Elton lived two doors down at 19 Clifton Hill and in 1761 the elder Isaac, Abraham's brother, had a house in Queens Square where he entertained the Duke of York, brother of King George III; 'After dinner to a ball at the Assembley Rooms. His Royal Highness opened the ball with Miss Elton, the Mayor's daughter...supped at the Mayor's and slept there.' The Brickdales lived at Rodney House and in 1775 Matthew Brickdale lived at 9 Clifton Hill. His father John was a partner of Isaac Hobhouse and co-owner of the *Loyal George* which on one occasion carried 220 slaves to Barbados.

Their god-fearing households, however, required a church in the rapidly growing suburb and St. Andrews was built to serve these residents. Some of the slave traders were churchwardens; the Eltons and Hobhouses had family pews. The records of the church include several references to the births, marriages and deaths of Negro slaves who lived in the new great houses.[24]

One tragic story recorded in the registers of St. Andrews concerned the baptism on 25 March 1723 of Francis Bristol, a Negro. On the 28 March a further entry recorded that he was 'in extreme danger of death', and that he was baptised by the request of Francis Creswick, his owner, Lord of the Manor of Hanham Abbots. The boy Francis died on 7 April and his burial completes his entry at St. Andrews.[25] Another record was that of the Negro Edward Peter Scipio who was also baptised 'in case of extreme danger of death' on 17 April 1724; his burial was recorded, but on 12 May 1730, six years later.[26]

The builders and owners of the new houses still lived in close proximity to the previous inhabitants, the labourers. The church records of St. Andrews clearly show the social divergence, from the baptism of George Usk, the 'Negro servant' of Walter Jenkins, a notable slave trader, to the burial of 'the Black Woman's child from ye limekilns' in August 1733.[27]

One of the earliest developments in central Bristol was in Queen Square, planned and built between 1694 and 1712 and named in honour of Queen Anne. Some plots were bought by builders who intended to build properties for rent, some by merchants who built their own houses. In 1727 for example, apart from the Custom House at No. 1, you would have found Abraham Elton's family living at No. 16, and Nathaniel Day at No. 29. Other early builders were Stephen Peloquin, the Huguenot merchant, and Captain Woodes Rogers.[28] The Eltons also built No. 12 St. James's Barton, with the house probably designed by John Strahan who also drew up the plans for Prince Street. Jacob Elton leased a new house in Queen Charlotte Street that had been erected by house carpenter and speculative builder, John Price.

Orchard Street, built between 1715 and 1718, also had its crop of mercantile property owners, many of them with connections to the Africa trade. William Swymmer owned No. 10, John Becher built Nos. 27 and 28, Andrew Ruddock lived at No. 29 and Alexander Neale at No. 18 – the latter may well have been the owner of the slave Rebecca Neale who married William Rice, also a slave.[29] From 1700 onwards, the development of Prince Street also attracted the Africa merchants: John Becher and Noblett Ruddock built there, the latter living at No. 66.[30] No. 40 was built in 1741 for Richard Bayly on the site of the 'Great House' of that Merchant Prince John Day, who had sold it in 1738.[31]

In 1718, Guinea Street was built on land belonging to the estate of Captain

Edmund Saunders, a prominent Guinea merchant – in 1730, for example, he was the agent for the *Aurora* gally, taking 370 slaves to Barbados. Part of the street (Nos. 10, 11 and 12) had been the site of the Saunders mansion; now there were 11 houses, a description of one of which has survived in the sales brochure of 1746:

> *'Four Vault Cellars, two Kitchens, a large handsome Hall, Dining-Room, and Withdrawing Room, each neatly Wainscotted and Painted, with a Marble Chimney-Piece in Each; three Parlours, two of them with Marble Chimney-Piece, all neatly Wainscotted, one of them with Cedar and Mahogany and highly finished; a very neat Mahogany Staircase, handsomly Painted, three Chambers Wainscotted, and a Marble Chimney-Piece in Each; with convenient Presses for Clothes, and three Closets. And six Upper Lodging-Rooms and two Closets, &c.'* [32]

This house had a quantity of features made of mahogany, the imported wood that became so fashionable from 1720 onwards. In 1721 the Government had passed an Act abolishing the heavy import duties on timber from North America and the West Indies, predominantly to fill a need for ship-building timber. This was part of the policy of Sir Robert Walpole and his government, 'to make the exportation of our own manufactures and the importation of the commodities used in the manufacturing of them as practicable as may be.' Builders and furniture-makers, as well as shipwrights, also benefited. In 1720 imports of mahogany were valued at £43; by 1722 this figure had risen to £277. In 1724 the sum was £1,237, in 1735, £6,430 and by 1750 the annual import value had risen to an incredible £30,000. Mahogany was an ideal wood for furniture and house decoration. It had a range of colours that would improve with the patina of age, it was strong and suited the elaborately carved furniture of the period, it provided wide boards (useful for building boards and large items of furniture) and resisted decay. [33]

The Harfords congregated in the new houses in King Square, built in the 1730s. This is partially explained by the designer, George Tully, being married to a Miss Harford. The couple lived in the Square themselves. [34] Neighbouring streets reflected the source of the wealth of the house owners – Jamaica Street and Carolina Street. Dighton Street referred to the Dighton family who had owned the land before it was developed.

An unknown local poet, published in *Felix Farley's Bristol Journal*, was less kind to the aspirations of those *nouveau riche* tradesmen who built their splendid new houses on the hill at Kingsdown:

> *'Each petty Tradesman here must have his Seat,*
> *And vainly think the Height will make him great;*
> *But little things look less the more they rise;*
> *So wrens may mount until they look like flies ...*

The wealth generated from the slave trade financed new houses, streets and crescents in the fashionable suburbs, particularly Clifton. From sketchbook, view of Clifton looking up from Clifton Wood towards St. Andrews Church (with some of the 'new' big houses), 1822. (Bristol's Museums, Galleries & Archives)

Come hither, Pedlars, quit your dusty stalls.
Here build your Seats, on rise your garden walls
And when you've built it o'er, call It what you will,
'Twill not be Kingsdown then, but Pedlars Hill. [35]

Daniel Defoe, in his *Tour* of 1769, wrote a scathing indictment of the Bristol merchants:

'The Merchants of Bristol, tho' very rich, are not like the Merchants of
London; the latter may be said (as of old of the Merchants of Tyre) to vie
with the Princes of the Earth; whereas the former, being rais'd by good
fortune, and Prizes taken in the Wars, from Masters of Ships, and blunt
tars, have inbib'd the Manners of those rough Gentlemen so strongly, that
they transmit it to their Descendants, only with a little more of the Sordid
than is generally to be found among British Sailors ... [36]

The Bristol newspapers, as always, listed sales of African slaves. *The Bristol Journal* of 23 June 1750 advertised for sale, 'a Negro Boy of about 12 years of age ... inquire at the printers.' The *Bristol Intelligencer* of 12 January 1754 offered for sale, 'newly landed, a lad of 14 years'. All the surviving advertisements are for young men: In August 1760 in *Felix Farley's Journal*, 'To be sold, a Negroe Boy about 10 years old. He has had the small pox'; in June 1767 in *The Bristol Journal*, 'To be sold, a Black Boy, about 15 years of age, capable of waiting at table'; in January 1768 in *Felix Farley's Bristol Journal*, 'A healthy Negro Slave named Prince, 17 years of age, extremely well grown; enquire of Joshua Springer in St Stephen's Lane'.

They also listed yet more 'elopements'. In March 1757, reported in *Felix Farley's Bristol Journal*, the slave of Captain Bouchier of Keynsham went missing; in September of 1757 it was the Negro slave of Captain Ezekiel Nash. In November 1746 in *Felix Farley's Journal*, Captain Eaton advertised the loss of his slave named Mingo, whom he had owned for eight years; Eaton offered a reward of one guinea for Mingo's return and added, 'All persons are hereby forbid entertaining the said Black at their peril.' In April 1759 in *Felix Farley's Bristol Journal* Captain Holbrook offered 'a handsome reward' for the return of his 'Negro man, named Thomas'. *The Bristol Journal* of March 1757 printed the disappearance of Starling, 'who blows the French horn very well.' His owner, a publican with premises in Prince's Street, offered one guinea reward for his return.

By a strange coincidence 30 years later, on 21 July 1787 Parson James Woodford, living at Weston Longueville Parsonage, Norfolk, was visited by a troop of travelling performers:

'This evening as we were going to Supper, a covered Cart drove into my
Yard with three Men with it, and one of them, the principal, was a black

Captain Kimber was accused of torturing and killing a 15-year-old African girl, a slave being taken on the Middle Passage. Although Kimber was acquitted the case became a 'cause celebre' and a powerful weapon in the abolition movement. Cartoon – Capt. Kimber and the slave girl. (National Maritime Museum)

*with a French Horn, blowing it all the way up the Yard to the Kitchen
Door, to know if we would like to see a little Woman only 33 Inches high
and 31 Years of Age. As we did not give our Dissent, she was taken out of
the Cart and brought into our Kitchen, where we saw her and heard her
sing two Songs…She was called by the Black Polly Coleshill of Gloster.
The Black told me that he formerly lived with the Earl of Albermarle. I
gave him 0.1.0.'* [37]

Where the name of the owner of a slave is mentioned, the title of captain is frequently mentioned. Captain Jacob Smith buried his servant Thomas Jamaica, 'a Christian Negro', in 1725 (he had been baptised the year before); Captain Martin's 'black', William Gloucester, was baptised in 1728. Captain Thomas Edwards arranged the baptism of his slave Alexander in 1730 and in 1744 Captain Joseph Smith and Captain Harman also had their black servants, John Ancoo and John Bristol, baptised.[38]

The reputations of the Captains of slaving ships seem to have been well known. In May 1768 an advertisement was placed in the *Bristol Journal* by Captain John Read. He wished to inform the public that the rumour that he had murdered his Negro servant and sold his body to Dr. Thomas Mountjoy of Whiteshill for dissection was a lie. Captain Read was prepared to borrow his slave back from his new owner and make him available for anyone to see who doubted the captain's word, 'at the expense of returning to Frenchay (from London), and bringing the negro with him, notwithstanding he had made him the property of another person by sale,' and offered £10 for anyone who could furnish him with the name of the person who started this rumour who had libelled him and put him to so much trouble.[9]

Apart from the captains, other owners tended to be the wealthy and sometimes the Guinea and West Indian merchants themselves. Richard Eagles owned a five-year-old boy called Noah who was buried in 1729 at Temple Church.[40] A Mr. Watkins owned a Negro maid called Catharine who died in 1735[41] and Mr. Scandrett's black servant James Pitman was baptised at Trinity Church, Stapleton in 1737.[42]

Notes
1   Latimer, John, *The Annals of Bristol in the Eighteenth Century* (1970), p.249-50
2   Latimer, John, op cit, p.322
3   ibid p.440
4   Latimer, John, *The History of the Society of Merchant Venturers of the City of Bristol* (1903), p.182
5   Latimer, John, *The Annals of Bristol in the Eighteenth Century* (1970), p.271
6   Plimmer, Charlotte & Denis, *Slavery: The Anglo-American Involvement* (1973), p.48
7   Latimer, John, *The Annals of Bristol in the Eighteenth Century* (1970), p.271
8   Richardson, David (ed.) *Bristol, Africa and the 18th Century Slave Trade to America: Years of Expansion 1698-1729*, Vol.1 (1986), p.189
9   Richardson, David (ed.), op cit, p.89-90
10 Richardson, David, *The Bristol Slave Traders, A Collective Portrait* (1996), p.29
11 Latimer, John, op cit, p.402
12 Bristol Central Reference Library, Ref B4140, *Trade and Commerce I, A List of the Company of Merchants Trading with Africa*
13 MacInnes, David & Charles, *Bristol: A Gateway of Empire* (1968), p.310, 316
14 Marcy, Peter T, *Eighteenth Century Views of Bristol and Bristolians* (1966), p.15
15 Ison, Walter, *The Georgian Buildings of Bristol* (1978), p.90-1
16 Latimer, John, *The Annals of Bristol in the Eighteenth Century* (1970), p.118
17 Ison, Walter, op cit, p.95-105
18 ibid p.108-14
19 ibid p.93
20 McGrath, Patrick, *The Merchant Venturers of Bristol* (1975), p.102
21 Jones, Donald, *A History of Clifton* (1992), p.39-40
22 Jones, Donald, op cit, p.39
23 ibid p.47-9
24 ibid, p.97-8
25 Lindegaard, DP, *Bristol Roots: Black Bristolians in the 17th, 18th and 19th Centuries* (1990), p.12
26 Bristol Record Office, FCP/StA/R/1
27 Bristol Record Office, FCP/StA/R/1
28 Ison, Walter, op cit, p.141-9
29 ibid p.152-6
30 ibid p.161-4
31 ibid p.171-3
32 ibid p.156-7
33 Edwards, Ralph & Ramsey, LGG (eds), *The Early Georgian Period 1714-60* (1957), p.44
34 Ison, Walter, op cit, p.173-4
35 Marcy, Peter T, Eighteenth Century Views of Bristol and Bristolians, McGrath, Patrick (ed.), *Bristol in the Eighteenth Century* (1972), p.28]
36 Marcy, Peter T, Eighteenth Century Views of Bristol and Bristolians, McGrath, Patrick (ed.), *Bristol in the Eighteenth Century* (1972), p.29]
37 Woodforde, James, & Beresford, John (ed), *The Diary of a Country Parson 1758-1802* (1956), p.306
38 Bristol Record Office, FCP/StP&J/R/1; FCP/StAug/R/1; FCP/StA/R/1
39 Latimer, John, *The Annals of Bristol in the Eighteenth Century* (1970), p.384
40 Lindegaard, DP, op cit, p.32
41 Bristol Record Office, FCP/StAug/R/1
42 Lindegaard, DP, op cit, p.33

Orchard Street, Bristol, home of Alexander Neale, and slave woman Rebecca. Built between 1715 and 1718 Orchard Street had its crop of mercantile property owners, many of whom had connections with the Africa trade. (M.Manson)

NINE

The 1730s and 1740s covered the zenith of Bristol's involvement in the slave trade. From the turn of the 1740s Bristol ships recorded fewer trips to Africa and concentrated on direct trade with the West Indies, so that the city's active participation in slave trading began to decline. From some 45% of the Africa trade, Bristol's share fell to around 25% in the early 1750s, 10% by the mid-1770s, and only 2% at the turn of the century – a fact that certainly helped prepare the way for Abolition.[1] The reasons for the decline were many and varied and included:

- The Governments of the West Indies and the American colonies sought greater control over their own trade in ways that disadvantaged the British Government and merchants
- A series of wars involved England and hit its maritime trade
- The American War of Independence closed the American markets for years
- The ships on the Triangular Trade found it increasingly difficult to buy slaves, and to find crews for the ships
- Insurance costs rose (taking into account enemy navies, privateers, pirates, sickness, and natural disasters)
- Bristol merchants suffered a series of financial disasters
- Liverpool overtook Bristol as the leading port in the slave trade
- Moral outrage was growing against trading in human beings

JAMAICAN LEGISLATION

The Jamaican legislature had been unhappy for many years about the terms of the slave trade that favoured the British-based trader over the local purchaser. As early as 1731, they had set a tax of 15s on each imported slave and 30s on each one that was subsequently re-exported. The tax was partly intended to raise revenue and partly to control the number of slaves coming into the Island – there was a fear that the white population would be swamped by African immigrants. In 1774 two Acts were passed to restrict or at least control the trade. Bristol, now joined by Liverpool, lobbied Parliament strongly to have the Acts rejected; the President of the Board of Trade answered the colonists' protests by stating, 'we cannot allow the colonists to check or discourage in any degree a traffic so beneficial to the nation.'[2] Undeterred, in 1775 the

Jamaican Assembly passed a law setting a duty on the import of all Negroes over the age of 30. Bristol's MP, Burke, in protest called it 'a very great duty'.[3]

Jamaica still needed some 6,000 slaves each year and by 1774 the annual cost of purchasing them had risen dramatically to about £360,000. One of the complaints by plantation owners was that middle men were buying the slaves and then leasing them to less well-off planters for £8-12 a year. This meant that the agent made a handsome profit but the planter had to pay each year for his slaves and had to reimburse the agent if they died whilst in his employ.[4]

Despite the problems of government, the plantation owners still maintained their close connection with England, to the point of naming estates and districts with English (and some Bristolian) titles. Thus Jamaica had plantations called Clifton Hill and Stapleton Mount. Newspapers in England, including the Bristol press, wrote about West Indian matters (offering plantations for sale, for example) and West Indian newspapers carried advertisements from Bristol companies (Chipping Sodbury Grammar School advertised for pupil boarders).[5] Many of the planters were to return to and/or settle in Bristol when they fulfilled a desire to return 'home'. In the 1720s, for example, Harrington Gibbs had lived in Jamaica and made the acquaintance of a number of the planters so that he was able to return to Bristol in 1726 and become the agent for the sale of their sugar. Gibbs' business would eventually be carried on by Mr. Atkins and his nephew John Curtis, both of whom had lived in Jamaica. The Messrs. Daniel Snr. and Jnr. returned from Barbados and set up in business dealing in Barbadian imports.

WARS

During the 18th century Britain was involved in a series of European and trans-Atlantic wars, all of which hit maritime trade. The Royal Navy was unable to provide ships to guard merchantmen when there were naval campaigns to be fought. The navies and privateers of enemy nations were happy to sink or seize English merchant ships, which disrupted trade and reduced England's wealth.

The century opened with the War of the Spanish Succession (1701-14). Four years later, England and France were once again at war with Spain; in 1729 a peace was declared with the Treaty of Seville. The War of the Austrian Succession was fought between 1740 and 1748; the Seven Years War raged from 1756 to 1763, the American War of Independence broke out in 1776 and the French Revolution and Napoleonic Wars took place from 1793 to 1815.

Conflict with Spain was frequent during the first half of the 18th century and culminated in The War of the Austrian Succession. As early as 1725 a Bristol ship, the

Anna Maria, owned by Lionel Lynde, had been seized by Spanish coastguards as she left Jamaica. This and other similar cases had persuaded the Society of Merchant Venturers to form a Committee to petition Parliament with a list of grievances concerning Spanish assaults on their shipping; it was complaints such as these that helped precipitate war in 1739.[6]

THE AMERICAN WAR OF INDEPENDENCE

The American War of Independence brought ruin to Bristol in many ways, not just with regard to the cessation of the trade in slaves. England had enjoyed a vast and lucrative trade with the 13 colonies (in 1764 52 ships sailed for America, 53 for the West Indies, and only 32 for Africa)[7] but this was to decline and virtually cease for many years. From 1774 onwards, Bristol companies making goods for America, like serge cloth and clay tobacco pipes, lost their markets as the American colonists sought to break away from the Mother Country. One example was a Bristol cloth trader who was able, each year, to buy about 3,000 pieces of cloth from Wiveliscombe for export to America; in 1774, this fell to 200 pieces and the following year the trade ended altogether.[8]

One of the issues raised in slave trading with Britain was that the American slave-states always maintained they got the worst of the slave cargoes. It was the custom of British ships, having unloaded the best of the slaves in the West Indies, to take the remainder (often old, sick or too young) on to America. Olaudah Equiano, then a sickly child, was taken firstly to Jamaica and when he was not sold, he was shipped on, with other unsold slaves, to South Carolina, where he eventually found a buyer. Another slave trading problem that arose with independence was that prior to 1775 American ships trading with Africa would carry British papers and fly British flags, putting them under the protection of the British Navy. However, once war broke out, American traders found it more difficult and hazardous to trade on the African coast under their own colours. British traders were as active as ever, but were now supplying Spanish and Portuguese colonies in South and Central America rather than the United States.[9]

On the other hand, the British were not too thrilled about the American practice of taking their surplus slaves to sell in the West Indies, only accepting gold or silver in exchange, then using the cash to purchase French or Spanish sugar which was cheaper than British.[10]

Like the West Indian islands, the colonies had set up taxes on slave imports to try and regulate the trade and make a profit for the local government. In 1723 Virginia set a tax of 40s a head on imported slaves and in 1757 they set a 20% duty on slaves into Virginia. As a result, slaves were imported into neighbouring Maryland, so that in 1761 this duty was removed.[11] By 1735 South Carolina had also set up a similar import tax, so that the *Amoretta* (Joseph Iles & Co, Master David Jones) out of Bristol had to pay import duty of £2,370 on 235 adults and 4 children, £20 for each adult and £5 for each child.[12] In 1766-8 they imposed an even higher tax which virtually stopped the import of slaves during this period. In 1751, for example, the *Delight* out of Bristol brought in 160 slaves, with import duty on the cargo of £1340; in 1769 the *King George* brought in 144 slaves (120 adults and 30 children) with a duty paid of £1440.[13]

The Bristol merchants, trading across the Atlantic, lobbied Parliament in 1775, even as war seemed inevitable. The petitions were addressed to the Cabinet, and begged that the Acts that forbade trade with the rebellious colonies should be repealed. In fact, this appeal was ignored and Bristol ships, along with those of other ports, were forced by a British blockade to return from America without having delivered their cargoes. The Merchant Venturers were joined in their protests by the West Indian merchants, who saw their trade with America likewise ruined – for example, they sold 20,000 hogsheads of sugar to America each year. Not only that, but the West Indies imported food and timber from the American states, which were important to their survival. Buying the same goods from England or Europe would cost more and take longer to deliver.[14]

The accounts of John Pinney from Nevis show that the cost of timber soared between 1768 and 1783, partly due to their having to be brought from England and Ireland, rather than from America. White oak staves for hogsheads [barrels] soared from a minimum of 60s to a maximum of 660s a thousand during this period. Some planters, with increased costs of food, allowed their slaves to fall into starvation and several hundred died during the year of the Revolution; some 700 died on Nevis alone. In June 1777 John Pinney wrote to his uncle:

> *'Our situation is truly alarming. What with the shortness of our present crop, and the low ebb of West-India credit, united with our present unhappy contest, will reduce many a worthy family to misery, and want... Enemies all around ! While at breakfast, a few weeks ago, I saw a brig taken, bound for St. Christopher, near my own landing. After the sailing of our last fleet, we shall be unhappily situated – subject to be pilfered and robbed by pirates in the night, who may, with ease, carry off our slaves, to the utter ruin of the planter... Provisions and all plantation necessaries are so excessively dear, that the expense of supporting our slaves and keeping up our estates in a proper condition, swallows up the greatest part of our produce.'* [15]

A minor irritation was that the loss of the American colonies and the dangers of travelling to the West Indies meant that transporting felons became difficult. In

John Pinney, who lived at the Georgian House in Great George Street, was a West Indian merchant and planter. He returned to Bristol in 1785 to retire. (Private owner; on loan to Bristol's Museums, Galleries & Archives)

October 1786 two Bristol women were recommended for pardon as they had been in prison for 3 years, awaiting transportation. It was lucky for the authorities that in Spring 1787 the first convicts could be sent to the newly discovered Botany Bay in Australia. In June 1789, according to the city's civic accounts, Daniel Burge received £83 1s 6d for 'what he advanced in London to pay the passage of 9 female convicts to New South Wales and his charges thereon'.[16]

From 1787 to 1800 7,547 convicts were shipped from England to Australia on 41 ships (convicts were packed at a rate of 0.5 person per ton, rather than the 1.6 persons per ton for slaves). The voyage to Australia lasted, on average, about 7 months. The mortality rate was 10.4%, which was about the same as the rate of slave ships whose voyages lasted about 3 months. Between 1810 and 1815, however, the rate improved. Some 8,778 convicts were transported on 55 ships and the mortality rate fell to 4.1%. After 1820 the rate fell to about 1% or less. The late 18th century mortality rate of about 10% was also common to emigrant ships from Europe but the people on board these ships, comprising as they did entire families, tended to contain a significant proportion of the very young, very old and very sick. Slaves, on the other hand, tended to be young and fit, and convicts tended not to include too many infants or frail and elderly people.[17]

The Government, backed by King George III, were adamant, however, that the rebellion in America could be crushed; they were not prepared to accept that trade would be so comprehensively ruined in what they envisaged would be a short skirmish. In Bristol, the citizens were not so sanguine; as people found their jobs disappearing and companies failing, the Poor Rate soared and many people were reduced to poverty. This did not prevent some local government supporters from lobbying the Mayor to record the city's support for the King and Cabinet's actions. A public meeting was held and a petition was duly forwarded to the King supporting his position, although, needless to say, a number of American and West Indian merchants refused to have anything to do with it. The Bristol M.P. Edmund Burke tried to introduce a Bill into Parliament that might lead to reconciliation, even at the eleventh hour, but it was vehemently rejected by the House.

Edmund Burke was MP for Bristol from 1774-80 and did not endear himself to the electorate – partly because he seldom visited Bristol. On this as on other occasions, he failed to speak on behalf of one section of the electorate as he was strongly pro-American, so that he only served one term as Bristol's MP. He was, however, famous in Parliament as an orator where his fiery Irish temper and theatrical style made him a powerful speaker.[18]

Interestingly enough, another of Bristol's MPs (from 1774-81), one who was to speak on the city's behalf in opposing Abolition, was Henry Cruger, a native of New York, who had come to Bristol to take on the English end of the family business. He married Ellen, daughter of Samuel Peach, a partner in Peach, Fowler & Co, Bank.[19] In 1790 Cruger returned to America and eventually became a Senator for New York State – making him possibly the only man ever to have been an American

Senator and an English MP.

Late in 1775 the Americans had sent out a number of privateers that attacked British shipping on the western side of the Atlantic and closer to home, off the British coast. War was inevitable. Not only was Bristol's trade with America in ruins, but now her trade with the rest of the world was threatened. In the case of the African trade, Bristol ships were pretty well moth-balled; those still trading with the West Indies ran a terrible risk. The House of Lords were told that in 1778, 247 ships trading with the Indies had been taken by American privateers – many of the ships lost came from Bristol.[20] However, Richard Champion, America merchant and porcelain manufacturer, was able to keep his business with America going by re-routing his exports through Holland.[21]

It is ironic that one of the most complete surviving records of a slaving voyage should come from these years. The accounts book of the *Africa*, detailing two voyages in 1775 and 1776, are the best record existing of this trade. They give full details – of the trade goods placed on board, both to use on the African coast to trade for slaves and to sell in the West Indies; the name and post of the crew members, the names of the merchants who paid for the trip, the tradesmen who supplied the trade goods and the supplies for the ship itself. Sadly, on the next voyage in 1776 the *Africa* met with an American privateer and was blown up.[22]

After the American War of Independence, some notable Boston families who had remained loyal to the British Crown emigrated to England and ended up in Bristol – among them, the Hutchinsons, Waldos, Vassalls, Van Schaaks and Hallowells.[23] Other exiles passed out of North America northwards. In October 1781 General Guy Carleton offered safe passage to 2,997 Virginian slaves who had fled to the British lines during the War. Faced with demands from the Virginian government for their return, Carleton loaded them on board the sloop *Bonnetta* and sailed for Halifax, Nova Scotia, where the people were landed. Despite repeated demands from Virginia for their return, the ex-slaves lived in Nova Scotia for some years. However, they found the climate difficult to bear and the attitudes of the some of the locals just as frosty. In March 1792 more than 1100 of the Virginian slaves were given passage to Sierra Leone, then under the governorship of Lieutenant John Clarkson, the brother of Thomas Clarkson the abolitionist.[24]

Meanwhile, once peace was established, American ships were again involved in slaving, now without any consideration of British involvement. Cargoes of slaves arrived in Charleston, Carolina, and Savannah, Georgia, very soon after. The American War of Independence was fought on a platform of freedom and in New England the idea was first voiced claiming that same freedom for African slaves. It would take many decades for that concept to become a reality.[25]

As in England, the Quakers were in the forefront of the call for Abolition. Their most prolific colonies were in Pennsylvania and Rhode Island (one of the leading slaving centres in the late 18th century). In 1761 the Pennsylvania legislature introduced a tax on imported slaves so high that it virtually wiped out the trade. In

1778 Virginia officially closed its ports to slave ships and in 1783 Maryland did the same. In 1786 North Carolina also introduced a prohibitive import tax, followed a year later by South Carolina. In that same year Rhode Island legislature passed a law forbidding slave trading by its citizens and the Quakers in America reported that not a single one of their number now owned a slave.[26]

As early as 1773 the Quakers had passed a rule that their members should try and free any slaves they owned, which was followed in 1784 by a rule that no Friend should own slaves at all. The first full-time school for Negro children was founded in Philadelphia by the Quaker Anthony Benezet. The Quakers found it easier than most to stick to their principles. They were used to being considered social oddities, holding views that were unpopular with outsiders, and cared nothing for the opinion of others. They spurned the luxuries that wealth provided so they had less need of slave labour to make them huge sums of money.[27]

Of course, not everyone shared the Quaker beliefs. Slavery was now so necessary to the economy, particularly in the Southern States, that a flourishing black market sprang up to supply those whose businesses, farms and plantations could not function without slave labour. Cheating the British government had become second nature during the latter part of British rule, and it just carried on. There was no effective State police force to stop anyone who was determined. One estimate suggests that in the 1760s and 1770s, c.66,000 slaves were brought into the United States; in the 1780s this figure rose to c.75,000 per annum. In the 1790s, after most of the anti-slavery legislation was passed, the figure fell slightly to c.69,000, but after 1800 it soared to meet demand. In the 8 years between 1800 and 1808, c.6,000,000 slaves were brought into the United States, often in direct breach of existing laws.[28]

There is an interesting theory that the southern landowners aspired to form a class like the landed gentry at home in Europe. Unfortunately, they had no peasantry to patronise. The native Indians were unsuitable and the poorest European was a freeman who owned land and therefore saw himself as potentially the equal of any wealthy landowner. They would not play at tugging the forelock. The African slaves filled the social gap; the owner could adopt the façade of paternalistic care and demand adoring subservience in return. The idea of freedom was unthinkable, as the ex-slave would then be able to own land and would no longer consider himself a grateful dependent. It was considered better that the slaves remain in servitude, adopting the role that the landowner wished them to play.[29]

Edmund Ruffin, a 19th century southerner, offered another reason for continuing the slave trade; 'one of the great benefits of the institution of African slavery to the Southern states is its effect in keeping away from our territory, and directing to the north and north-west, the hordes of immigrants now flowing from Europe.'[30] Whether this disinclination to come south was from lack of employment or disgust, Ruffin does not make clear.

DIFFICULTY IN BUYING SLAVES

The availability of slaves was becoming a serious problem. The population of the coastal areas had already been substantially reduced and now it became harder and more time-consuming to bring together a cargo of viable slaves. A letter from a Liverpool slaver to his principal, written from Old Calabar in August 1767, sums up the situation:

> *'There are now seven vessels in the river, each of which expects to purchase 500 slaves, and I imagine there was seldom ever known a greater scarcity of slaves than at present. The natives are at variance with each other, and in my opinion it will never be ended before the destruction of all the people in Old Town [Calabar], who have taken the lives of many a fine fellow. The river of late has been very fatal. There have been three Captains belonging to Bristol died within these few months, besides a number of officers and sailors.*[31]

At the end of 1790 the *Pearl* out of Bristol was obliged to wait more than 9 months in Old Calabar before she loaded a sufficient cargo of slaves. The result was as expected, with a high mortality rate amongst both slaves and crew.[32] Earlier, in 1764 the *Black Prince* (Captain William Miller) spent the time from October 1764 to March 1765 trading on Cape Mount. The local agent confirmed that supply 'for these many months, has been miserable indeed; so very bad, that poor old Miller (who you know always brings good cargoes) has been here six months and has not purchased 20 slaves'.[33]

Eventually areas like Senegambia cut back on slaving altogether. The slave sellers could not find a buyer even for the pitiful few they could assemble, especially when they asked too much for them, so that ships were leaving the African coast without a single slave in the hold. The traders were also no longer ready to accept the standard European goods – a copper pot and a couple of handfuls of glass beads were no longer enough to buy a slave. So much material had poured into Africa that it had lost a great deal of its value. Greater and greater quantities of merchandise were needed to make a purchase and anyway the chiefs could trade directly with merchants in North Africa for the same goods. The role of the European trader was becoming of less importance to the African economy.

Notes
1   Richardson, David, *The Bristol Slave Traders: A Collective Portrait* (1985), p.3
2   Thompson, Vincent Bakpetu, *The Making of the African Diaspora* (1987), p.207
3   Latimer, John, *The History of the Society of Merchant Venturers* (1903), p.184
4   Latimer, John, *The Annals of Bristol in the Eighteenth Century* (1970), p.413-4
5   Little, Bryan, *The City and County of Bristol* (1967), p.160-1
6   McGrath, Patrick, *The Merchant Venturers of Bristol* (1975), p.139
7   McGrath, Patrick, op cit, p.141
8   Latimer, John, *The Annals of Bristol in the Eighteenth Century* (1970), p.414
9   Duigan, Peter & Clendenen, Clarence, *The United States and the African Slave Trade 1619-1862* (1963), p.12
10   Plimmer, Charlotte & Denis, *Slavery: The Anglo-American Involvement* (1973), p.9
11   Richardson, David, (ed), *Bristol, Africa and the 18th Century Slave Trade to America: The Years of Decline 1746-68*, Vol.3 (1991), p.xxvi
12   Richardson, David (ed.) *Bristol, Africa and the 18th Century Slave Trade to America: Years of Ascendancy 1730-1745*, Vol.2 (1987), p.60]
13   Richardson, Davis, Bristol, *Africa and the 18 Century Slave Trade to America: The Years of Decline 1746-69*, Vol.3 (1991), p.45, 232
14   Latimer, John, op cit, p.415
15   Pares, Richard, *A West-Indian Fortune* (1968), p.91-3
16   Latimer, John, op cit, p.470
17   Klein, Herbert S, *The Atlantic Slave Trade* (1999), p.134
18   Underdown, PT, 'Bristol and Burke', McGrath, Patrick (ed.), *Bristol in the Eighteenth Century* (1972), p.45-62
19   Cave, Charles Henry, *A History of Banking in Bristol 1750-1899* (1899), p.102
20   Latimer, John, op cit, p.416
21   Little, Bryan, op cit, p.162
22   Richardson, David, *Bristol, Africa and the 18th Century Slave Trade to America: The Final Years 1770-1807*, Vol 4, (1996), p.70
23   Little, Bryan, op cit, p.162-3
24   McColley, Robert, *Slavery and Jeffersonian Virginia* (1964), p.84
25   Duigan, Peter & Clendenen, Clarence, *The United States and the African Slave Trade 1619-1862* (1963), p.13
26   Duigan, Peter & Clendenen, Clarence, op cit, p.13-5
27   McColley, Robert, op cit, p.153-4
28   Klein, Herbert S, op cit, p.45
29   McColley, Robert, op cit, p.54
30   Plimmer, Charlotte & Denis, *Slavery: The Anglo-American Involvement* (1973), p.7
31   Latimer, John, *Annals of Bristol in the Eighteenth Century* (1970), p.380
32   Richardson, David (ed.), *Bristol, Africa and the 18th Century Slave Trade to America: The Final Years 1770-1807* (1991), Vol.4, p.172
33   Richardson, David, (ed), *Bristol, Africa and the 18th Century Slave Trade to America: The Years of Decline 1746-68*, Vol.3 (1991), p.171

TEN

HARD TO GET CREWS - THE MIDDLE PASSAGE EXPOSED

The Triangular Trade was notorious for its danger and cruelty, so much so that sailors preferred any berth to one on a slaver. In 1787, according to the city's Muster Rolls, 554 seamen were employed on 23 ships trading to West Africa and thence across the Atlantic; 100, or 18%, were reported to have died during the journey. Of the 55 voyages going straight to the West Indies, out of 1,151 crewmen, 21, or 5.5%, died. Ships going to other destinations totalled 125, and only 3 seamen out of 1,133 were recorded as having died *in transit*.[1] When Clarkson presented his case against the slave trade to the Board of Trade in 1788, he quoted figures for the number of deaths of seamen sailing on Bristol shipping on 27 July 1784; they listed the location and the number dead per thousand: Greenland 10, Newfoundland and St. Petersburg each 11, West Indies 23, East India 41 – the slave trade 219.[2]

A perfect example of the kind of voyage that discouraged seamen from taking a berth on a slaver was that of the *Britannia*, which sailed from Bristol to Guinea in 1762. The second stage of the voyage was held up by bad weather and only 9 of the 44 crew and 239 of the 300 slaves, survived to reach St. Kitts; when the ship finally docked in Jamaica, 4 of the 44 crew remained alive.[3]

There were other drawbacks. Although they might be promised large wages, when the ship reached the West Indies or North America, crewmen were paid half their salary in the local currency – Jamaican pounds, for example, rather than English ones. As the foreign currencies were worth less than the English pound, the sailors lost out considerably, especially if the ship was held up in the West Indies waiting for a return cargo. In that case, they would have to spend most of their wages just to live until the return voyage. An example of the divergence is given from the sale of slaves from the *Mathilda* in 1754; at South Carolina the slaves fetched £35 sterling = £260-70 local.[4] Some captains turned their crews loose on shore and after 48 hours any who had not returned were declared to have deserted and were not allowed back on board. They were left to live off what they had already been paid and denied the balance of their pay for the return journey to Bristol. The Royal Commission on the Slave Trade, sitting in 1789, was told by the seaman, William Jones, of this happening with the crews of the *Bristol* and the *Juno*. Slave ships always required a higher number of crew members to tend and guard the slaves and it made good financial sense to get rid of some of them, as they would be superfluous on the trip home, either empty or with a regular cargo.[5]

So hard was it to get a crew that captains were obliged to hire African crew members to cover the Triangular Trade route. This cannot have been an easy choice for an African seaman to make; apart from the usual problems of low pay, vile conditions and cruelty, an African ran the additional risk of being sold himself when the ship docked. In 1755 the *Ulysses* signed on an African and an Indian to the crew in Bristol; both were later sold in Jamaica.[6]

In 1747 an Act was passed 'For the Relief and Support of Mariners and Disabled Seamen, and the Widows and Children of such as shall be killed, slain or drowned in the Merchants Service'. The result was the setting up of the Seamen's Hospital Fund, to which all seamen contributed 6d a month when they were employed. In Bristol, the Society of Merchant Venturers administered the Seamen's Hospital Fund that provided financial support for seaman and officers and their dependants who had fallen on hard times. The records of the Fund give a number of examples of the claims being made by those in the Guinea and West Indian Trade.[7]

One major risk for seamen was loss of sight through illness. In December 1753 John Fling, a seaman on the *Black Prince*, was awarded £8 a year after losing his sight during the voyage from Africa to Virginia. In January 1761 Thomas Dilliston, a 15-year old boy, was blinded 'by a distemper which rag'd amongst the slaves' whilst the ship was moored on the Bonny River and awarded 2s 6d a week with an additional 40s to help him get to his uncle's house in Ipswich. A similar fate had befallen Cornelius Calahan in September 1767 on a voyage from Calabar to Jamaica; he was given a pension of £6 10s per annum, 15s to pay his landlord what was owed and 10s to get him home to Tralee in Ireland.[8]

A particularly interesting case occurred in 1755. Robert Barker had sailed as carpenter aboard the *Thetis*, for Africa and the West Indies. During the voyage, Barker made a complaint about the food to the captain, Robert Wapshutt and was accused of incitement to mutiny and locked up in chains. As a result, he fell ill with 'a distemper then raging amongst the slaves' and lost his sight. When he got back to Bristol, he claimed from the Seamen's Hospital Fund, who awarded him 3s 6d a week. Apart from this, Barker sued Wapshutt and won £26 in damages in February 1758. He then went on to write a pamphlet entitled *'The Unfortunate Shipwright, or Cruel Captain, being a Faithful Narrative of the Unparalleled Sufferings of Robt. Barker, late Carpenter on board the 'Thetis' snow of Bristol in a Voyage to the Coast of Africa and Antigua'.* In December 1760 the Hospital Trustees had read the booklet and decided that he had '... inserted several falsehoods calculated to Blacken the Character of Persons who appear to be innocent, and to raise the Compassion on his behalf and to get money as an Unfortunate Seaman.' The Trustees cancelled his pension, whether because he had genuinely libelled anyone, or to punish him for taking action against the Captain (and winning), is not known.[9]

Widows and orphans also applied – Ann Hancock was the 2-year-old daughter of a sailor on the *Juba*, killed during a slave revolt; her nurse was given 10s for 'present needs', and a recommendation was made that Ann should apply again when she had found a settled home. In January 1769 the widow of James Harding of the *Speedwell* applied for help; her husband had been 'poisoned by Blacks whilst the said ship was on the Coast of Africa'. She and her two children presented a certificate as to their circumstances signed by the Minster and Churchwardens of St. Michael's Church. A joint request was recorded in June 1765, when the widows of Commander John Westcott and the Mate Thomas Flood of the sloop *William*, requested support since their husbands had been 'Murdered and thrown overboard by the Sailors' on the voyage from Africa to St. Christopher's. Not only the widows and orphans of seamen could apply to the Merchant Venturers. In 1756 Mrs. Benedicta Henville, widow of Richard Henville, an ex-Master of the Society of Merchant Venturers, was awarded an annual pension of £30, whilst £10 per annum had been awarded in 1733 to Sarah Swymmer, the daughter of William Clarke, another Merchant Venturer.[10]

TROUBLE WITH VOYAGES – HIGH INSURANCE – FINANCIAL LOSSES – CREDIT

The cost of funding a voyage rose over the decades of the 18th century. In 1710 the average cost of fitting out a slaving ship would have been in the region of £2,500; by 1750 this sum had risen to around £5,000 and by the 1780s it increased to about £7,300.[11] As basic prices at home stayed relatively stable over the period, this meant that the cost of purchasing and transporting slaves grew enormously, helping to make slaving voyages less financially attractive. Slave traders tended to own their ships, rather than charter them; Slavers had to carry larger crews than ordinary merchant ships, they needed special equipment like chains, nets, food, medicines and fire-arms and over the years the price of a slave in trade goods rose substantially as demand remained steady but supply became more difficult. The actual purchase price of slaves is difficult to assess, depending on the value of the goods exchanged, cloth, metalwork, glass beads, cowrie shells, guns or rum. John Atkins, a naval surgeon, wrote from his observations concerning the slave trade:

'…Iron Bars which are not asked for to the Leeward [Coast] are a substantial part of Windward cargoes…as are brass pans from Rio Sesthos to Appolonia; cowreys at Whydah; copper and iron bars at Callabar; but Arms, Gun-Powder, Tallow…Cottons of all Denominations, and English Spirits are everywhere called for…'[12] Looking at the value of the cargo and how many slaves it was exchanged for, a rough calculation would mean that in the 1680s the average price for a slave (including men, women and children) was around £3.[13] Between 1728 and 1742 the price rose from £13 to

£17 for an adult male.[14] By the early 1760s the prices had doubled, in 30 years they had doubled again, and by 1800 they were five times higher than in 1700.

By no means all the slaving voyages made large profits; some even made substantial losses. In 1789 the *Sarah* lost 80 of her 222 slaves to 'flux and fever' on the journey from Bonny to Barbados. The final reckoning, after the ship had returned to Bristol, was that for an outlay of £6,135, the total proceeds were only £4,866.[15] The *Emperor*, sailing to South Carolina in 1754, was obliged by bad weather to divert to Jamaica. Of her cargo of 390 slaves (it had been hoped to load 570), 120 had died and the remainder were in bad shape, fetching low prices. The initial cost for outfitting the voyage and for the trade cargo had been £7,100 and the final loss on the voyage was £3,000.[16]

Not all the losses were from the death of slaves from the cargo. It was the practice for plantation owners to buy slaves on credit, making a deposit, then paying the balance within an agreed period. In 1740 Benjamin King and Robert Arbuthnot, agents for Isaac Hobhouse and Stephen Baugh in Antigua, wrote to their principals:

> 'We have no objection to the Bond you mention by way of Security, as it is a Beginning; but pray the favour of your next may be more favourable, 6/8ths Remitted by the Ships & ye other 2/8ths in twelve months being somewhat hard, Considering the Great & Long Credit given here, from which Credit a better price is allways obtain'd, & must Certainly turn to your advantage, the Diffrence being 3 or £4 ye Negro between Long & Short Credit or no Credit. We hope & pray it as a favour in your future affairs of this kind, you'd be Content with 5/8ths & other 3/8ths in Eighteen months, and wch we shall allways be very punctual in; and sh'd it be in our power to Remit the whole Directly, you need not doubt our Doing it, as we think it's a very unfair practice to keep other persons Effects, to serve other Ends as is often done.'[17]

Having purchased on credit, the plantation owners sometimes failed to pay the balance when it became due. This could be deliberate fraud, but more often it was due to some financial failure of the planter, or simply due to his having bought slaves in anticipation of a crop (and thus a profit) greater than that which would actually be harvested. Between 1730 and 1736, for example, there was a drop in the price of sugar which led to the failure of some planters and severe financial difficulties for others. When this happened, the Bristol merchant had to stand the loss, especially if the planter did not have assets that could be seized to settle the debt.[18]

Insurance was a problem. The premiums were high (indeed, rates from Bristol insurance companies were often higher than those of London firms); the agent either had to pay, or risk the loss of the ship without any hope of financial reimbursement. In 1761 the agents of the *Sally* (Captain James McTaggart; Agents, Henry Bright & Co.) took out £1000 worth of insurance, which cost them 12 guineas per £100; the policy failed to cover 'Mortality of Negroes by natural death'.[19] In 1785, for example, a ship carrying 225 slaves was subject to two separate mutinies. Nineteen of the slaves were killed by the crew and a further 36 died as a result of swallowing sea water when they jumped overboard as the mutinies failed. The agents put in a claim for all 55, only to have the insurance company agree to compensate them for the 19 who were killed, but not for the 36 who, it was judged, had not died as a direct result of the mutiny. If a slave died of natural causes (illness), the cost fell on the owner; if the slave died as a result of mutiny, or if they were intentionally thrown overboard whilst still alive, known as 'legal jettison', the insurance company would pay.[20]

Granville Sharp, the Abolitionist, was involved in the particularly vile case of the slave ship *Zong*. In 1781 the ship had sailed from Africa and because the trip took several months, the slaves became sick and therefore unlikely to sell. On 29 November 1781, 54 slaves were thrown into the sea whilst still alive. On 1 December another 42 were murdered in the same manner and 26 on 9 December. A further 10 jumped overboard of their own accord, rather than be bound or shackled and thrown into the sea like the others. Out of 440, some 60 had already died and the captain had 132 sick slaves thrown overboard to drown. He claimed to have done this on the grounds that the ship did not have enough water to keep them alive and it would be kinder to kill them outright rather than let them die slowly from thirst. This was a lie, as there was adequate water, supplemented by collected rainwater – the real reason was that the insurers would pay if the cargo were 'lost', but not if they were merely 'damaged'. As Granville Sharpe put it:

> '...the dead and dying slaves would have been a dead loss to the owners, in some proportion, a loss also to the persons employed by the owners, unless some pretence or expedient had been found to throw the loss on the insurers, as in the case of Jetsam or Jetson (Jettison) i.e. a plea of necessity to cast overboard some part of a cargo to save the rest.'[21]

In fact, the insurers refused to pay at all, saying that they were not liable for deaths resulting, in whatever degree, from illness. They argued that the slaves were killed because they were sick, not because their deaths were essential to the survival of the rest of the cargo. They would, of course, have paid if the slaves had been executed after rebelling (jetsam). The argument in court was based on the concept that slaves were property, not people, and should be assessed as such for insurance purposes.

BANKRUPTCIES AMONGST MERCHANTS

The merchants of Bristol, those directly and indirectly involved in the slave trade, both rose to wealth and aristocracy, and fell into total ruin. A typical example of the latter case was Graffin Prankard, a merchant who traded with the West Indies and America, as well as with Newfoundland, Europe and Ireland. He married Sarah, a cousin of Nathaniel Alloway, Master of the Merchant Venturers; their only daughter, Sarah, married Caleb Dickinson, a wealthy Jamaican plantation owner. Prankard's reputation and credit enabled him to build his own trading ships, the *Parham Pink* in 1724 and the *Baltick Merchant* in 1732, in the yard of Sydenham Teast. It would have seemed that he was unassailably successful but the loss of his two ships with their cargoes (one was not insured) led to his bankruptcy. It was only his son-in-law Dickinson and brother-in-law John Galton, who salvaged anything from the wreckage of his dealings; Prankard later surfaced as an agent in Jamaica, a far cry from his prominent position in Bristol.'[22]

William Champion was another merchant who fell foul of the moving market. He was a partner in the Warmley Copper Works where so many trade goods were made for the Triangular Trade; his partners were Thomas Goldney the banker, Thomas Crosby and his brother-in-law Sampson Lloyd. In addition to his successful Works, in the Seven Years War he part-owned a 100 ton privateer, the *Nancy*. He lived at Clifton Court, one of the impressive new houses high above the city. However, by 1769 he was bankrupt. Richard Farr Jnr., son of Richard Farr the rope-maker and slave trader, lived nearby in Clifton Wood House. He was a slave trader between 1747 and 1772, Master of the Merchant Venturers in 1762, Mayor of Bristol in 1763 – and bankrupt in 1778. Of his seven children, two of his sons, Thomas (Sheriff in 1762 and Mayor in 1775) and Paul (Master of the Merchant Venturers in 1775) both went bankrupt with him. Amongst other factors, the family company, Richard Farr & Co had suffered heavy losses during the American War of Independence; Thomas alone was owed £8,200 from debts raised by merchants from South Carolina which had to be written off.[23]

LIVERPOOL

Along with all the other troubles, Bristol found itself being rapidly overhauled by Liverpool in several areas of trade, a fact reported by David Macpherson, writing in 1805:

Wapping, Bristol, c.1760. Drawing, Nicholas Pococke, shows docks of Sydenham Teast. (Bristol's Museums, Galleries & Archives)

> *'There were entered inward this year [1765] at Bristol 384 British, and
> 47 foreign, vessels; and outward 319 British and 44 foreign. In Liverpool
> there were entered inward 1,738 British and 65 foreign vessels; and
> outward 795 British and 70 foreign... From these statements it appears
> that Liverpool had gained greatly upon Bristol, and was henceforth to be
> considered as the second port in Britain ...'* [24]

As early as 1753, a count of ships leaving the African coast was recorded as 64 from
Liverpool, 27 from Bristol, 13 from London, 7 from Lancaster, 4 from Glasgow, and
1 each from Chester and Plymouth.[25] In 1771, the Guinea Coast was visited by 107
ships from Liverpool, 58 from London, and 23 from Bristol.[26] Whilst Liverpool
picked up more of the trade with Jamaica and Barbados, Bristol managed to hold on
to the bulk of her trade with Antigua, St. Kitts and Dominica.[27]

The following quote comes from Mathews' *The New History, survey and
description of the city and suburbs of Bristol, or Complete Guide and Bristol Directory for the Year
1793-4:*

> *'The Ardor for the Trade to Africa for men and women, our fellow
> creatures and equals, is much abated among the humane and benevolent
> Merchants of Bristol. In 1787 there were but 30 ships employed in this
> melancholy traffic; while the people of Liverpool in their indiscriminate
> rage for Commerce and for getting money at all events have nearly
> engrossed this Trade, incredibly exceeded London and Bristol in it, employ
> many thousands of tons of shipping for the purposes of buying and
> enslaving God's rational creatures, and are the venders (horresco referns)
> of the souls and bodies of men and women to almost all the West Indies
> Islands!!!'* [28]

Various reasons were given for Liverpool's growth, as opposed to Bristol's decline.
Part of it was due to Liverpool offering lower port fees and having better dock
facilities. Bristol certainly recognised the problems with getting larger ships into the
centre of the city along the Avon Gorge, and plans were made and carried out during
the 18th century for better access and docking. In 1767 William Champion put
forward a plan to build a new floating harbour in the city centre. He had already built
Champion's Dock (now known as Merchant's Dock), and saw the need for a large
new facility. Politics took over and it was not until 1801-2 that William Jessop of
London was finally chosen to design the Floating Harbour for the Corporation and
Merchant Venturers. A Dock Company was formed and in 1804 work was started; it
was finished in 1809, at a cost of £600,000 – forty years after it was first needed.[29]

Notes
1   Press, Jonathan, *The Merchant Seamen of Bristol 1747-89* (1976), p.11
2   Curtin, PD, *The Atlantic Slave Trade, A Census* (1969), p.285
3   Richardson, David, (ed), *Bristol, Africa and the 18th Century Slave Trade to America: The Years of Decline 1746-68*, Vol.3 (1991), p.150
4   Richardson, David, (ed), op cit, p.84
6   Press, Jonathan, op cit, p.9
7   ibid, p.2
8   McGrath, Patrick, *The Merchant Venturers of Bristol* (1975), p.197-8
9   McGrath, Patrick, op cit, p.200-1
10   Press, Jonathan, op cit, p.19
11   McGrath, Patrick, op cit, p.201, 206
12   Richardson, David, *The Bristol Slave Traders: A Collective Portrait* (1985), p.6
13   Everett, Susanne, *History of Slavery* (1997), p.36
14   Klein, Herbert S, *The Atlantic Slave Trade* (1999), p.110
15   Richardson, David, *Bristol, Africa and the 18th Century Slave Trade to America: The Years of Ascendancy 1750-43* (1987), p.xxii
16   Richardson, David, (ed), *Bristol, Africa and the 18th Century Slave Trade to America: The Final Years 1770-1807*, Vol.4
17   Richardson, David, (ed), *Bristol, Africa and the 18th Century Slave Trade to America: The Years of Decline 1746-68*, Vol.3 (1991), p.80
18   Bristol Industrial Museum Collection Reg. No. J1600
19   Pares, Richard, *A West-Indian Fortune* (1968), p.250-1
20   Richardson, David, (ed), *Bristol, Africa and the 18th Century Slave Trade to America: The Years of Decline 1746-68*, Vol.3 (1991), p.147
21   Robinson, Derek, *A Shocking History of Bristol*, (1973) p.64
22   Plimmer, Charlotte & Denis, *Slavery: The Anglo-American Involvement* (1973), p.60
23   Bettey, JH, 'Graffin Prankard, an Eighteenth-Century Bristol Merchant, in Southern History', *A Review of the History of Southern England*, Vol 12, 1990
24   Jones, Donald, A History of Clifton (1992), p.46-7
25   Marcy, Peter T, 'Eighteenth Century Views of Bristol and Bristolians', McGrath, Patrick (ed.), *Bristol in the Eighteenth Century* (1972), p.16
26   McInnes, CM, 'Bristol and the Slave Trade', McGarth, Patrick (ed.), *Bristol in the Eighteenth Century* (1972), p.169
27   McInnes, C.M., 'Bristol and the Slave Trade', McGrath, Patrick (ed.), Bristol in the 18th Century (1972), p.169
28   Richardson, David, (ed), *Bristol, Africa and the 18th Century Slave Trade to America: The Years of Decline 1746-68*, Vol.3 (1991), p.xxx]
29   McInnes, CM, op cit, p.169-70
30   Minchinton, Walter, 'The Port of Bristol in the Eighteenth Century', McGrath, Patrick (ed.), *Bristol in the Eighteenth Century* (1972), p.139-40

ELEVEN

MORAL OUTRAGE

Apart from laws framed as a response to the needs of trade, there was a growing repugnance to slavery on moral grounds.

One of the greatest reformers was Granville Sharp (1735-1813) who was responsible for three well-publicised legal cases that helped to set the precedent for freedom of slaves in Britain. The first was put forward in 1767; a slave called Jonathan Strong had been savagely beaten by his owner, David Lisle, a London lawyer. Lisle had thrown Strong out of his house because he seemed to be dying, Strong went to a local doctor who happened to be Sharp's brother, William, and it was at the surgery that they met. Sharp got Strong admitted into St. Bartholomew's Hospital for 4 months and when he was well enough, got him a job. Strong's erstwhile owner saw him 2 years later, realised that he had recovered and arranged to have him kidnapped and sold to a West Indian plantation owner, James Kerr. Just before Strong was to be sent to the Indies, he managed to get a message to Sharp who went to court and had Kerr accused of kidnapping. The case was heard before the Lord Mayor of London who ruled that since Strong 'had not stolen anything and was not guilty of any offence' he was free to go. Infuriated at losing their property and money, Lisle challenged Sharp to a duel and Kerr sued him for the value of his lost property; Sharp refused to fight Lisle or to give in to Kerr who eventually dropped his case. Jonathan Strong, however, never fully recovered from his appalling treatment and he died in 1772, aged only 25.[1]

During this period, Sharpe made one of many impassioned pleas on behalf of Negro slaves:

> *'The plea of private property in a Negro, as in a horse or a dog, is very insufficient and defective ... They cannot be justified, unless they shall be able to prove that a Negro Slave is neither man, woman or child ... This poor Negro [Strong] has not been guilty of any offences, for which he might lawfully be divested of his humanity; and therefore, it must certainly be allowed that he differs from a horse or a dog in this essential point, viz. his humanity'* [2]

The year before Strong's death, Sharp had taken up another case, that of Thomas

Lord Chief Justice Mansfield, himself a slave owner, was loth to make any ruling that would acknowledge that a slave living in England was free by the very fact that the laws of England did not permit owning another person. Portrait of Lord Mansfield, by J.S.Copley, 1783. (National Portrait Gallery)

Lewis, a slave who had been kidnapped off the street by his former owner who had him taken on board a Jamaica-bound ship in chains. Once again, Sharp got to hear of this, arranged for a writ to be issued and thanks to bad weather delaying sailing, was able to rescue Lewis. Again, the case ended up in court, this time in front of Lord Mansfield, Lord Chief Justice. Mansfield, himself a slave owner, was loth to make any ruling that would acknowledge that a slave living in England was free by the very fact that the laws of England did not permit owning another person. He advised the jury, 'perhaps it is much better that it should never be discussed or settled ... I don't know what the consequences may be, if the masters were to lose their property by accidentally bringing their slaves to England.' The jury, however, decided that they believed Lewis was a free man who should not have been kidnapped and he was set at liberty.[3]

The third and most memorable case was that of the slave James Somerset, which came to court in December 1771. Once again, the slave in question had been kidnapped in London by his owner, Charles Steward, who had brought him to England from Virginia. Sharp took this case to court, his lawyers arguing that a man enslaved under Virginia law could not be held as a slave in England, since English law did not recognise the state of slavery – 'Have the laws of Virginia any more influence, power or authority in this country than the laws of Japan?'. In fact, he argued, just by coming under English law a slave was legally free. Mansfield was the judge for this case as well, and he made every effort to persuade Steward to back down and leave Somerset alone, to avoid having to draw the obvious legal conclusion; Steward, however, refused and Mansfield was obliged to make a ruling: 'A foreigner cannot be imprisoned here on the authority of any law existing in his own country ... No master was ever allowed here to take a slave by force to be sold abroad because he deserted from his service, or for any other reason.'[4]

Mansfield was very careful not to say that a slave arriving in England was automatically free. A slave could not be forced to leave England, but he was still his master's property.

These cases, and the affair of the *Zong*, were landmarks in anti-slavery legislation but it did not stop the ill-treatment of slaves and their being sent to the colonies against their wills – Mansfield had managed to avoid ruling that slavery was actually illegal in England. In 1790 Hannah Moore wrote to Horace Walpole:

> '*I cannot forbear telling you that at my city of Bristol, during church-time, the congregations were surprised last Sunday with the bell of the public crier in the streets. It was so unusual a sound on that day that the people were alarmed in the churches. They found that the bellman was crying the reward of a guinea to any one who would produce a poor Negro girl who had run away because she would not return to one of those trafficking islands, whither her master was resolved to send her. To my great grief and indignation, the poor trembling wretch was dragged out*

from a hole in the top of a house where she had hid herself, and forced on board ship.' 5

In December 1792 a similar kidnapping and forcing of a Negro woman on board a ship for Jamaica, was recorded in *Bonner's Bristol Journal*. The woman had been sold by her owner for £80 and according to the newspaper, 'A bystander who saw her put on board the boat at Lamplighter's Hall says, "Her tears flowed down her face like a shower of rain".' These acts were illegal, but they continued as long as the law did not interfere.

Once Granville Sharp intervened and publicised the case, there was so much public indignation that Parliament were obliged to consider the moral questions arising from the slave trade. They finally did pass an Act in 1788, regulating conditions on board slave ships, particularly the space to be allowed for each slave. The question became known as the tight vs. loose packing question. Loose packing involved taking fewer slaves, on the grounds that with more space, more of them would be likely to survive. Tight packing meant getting as many slaves as possible into the ship, with the result that, even if a substantial number of them died of ill-treatment, disease and melancholy, enough would survive to make the voyage profitable.

To get an idea of space per man, the *Mayflower*, taking the Pilgrim Fathers to America, was a vessel of 180 tons and carried 102 pilgrims. Amongst slave ships, the *Hector*, of 200 tons, carried 512 slaves on one voyage; the *Greyhound*, 120 tons, 410 slaves; the *Williamsburg*, 100 tons, 335 slaves; *The Bryce*, also 100 tons, 414 slaves; the *Tryal*, 90 tons, 356 slaves (and 390 on another occasion), and the *Bridget*, 70 tons, 225 slaves. The *Williamsburg*, in order to fit in more slaves, added a 'floor' in the hold, reducing headroom of 5 feet to two shelves with headroom of barely 2 feet 6 inches each.6

'Loose' packing did not always mean fewer deaths – in 1755, the *Emperor* out of Bristol, loaded 390 slaves, rather than the planned 570; the voyage was horrendous, and 120 slaves died. The *Nugent*, sailing from Gambia to South Carolina in 1754, was more successful, losing only 4 of her 208 slaves, who had been carried instead of the anticipated 250, and getting £240-260 (local) for each one. This was put down to the skill of the Captain, James Hutcheson, who was described by the Agent, John Guerard, as:

> '...a Prodigious Clever fellow [who] understands the Trade perfectly well and as he had the Start Commanded the Trade and would not Suffer any to do Business till he had Got what he Design'd. He Might have Compleated his full Number by Staying a Little Longer but Judged it more for his Owners Interest to Come Earlyer in the Season by which Conduct they'l Reap the Advantage.' 7

Merchants of London, Liverpool and Bristol financed lobbying to prevent this Bill, and the Bristol MP, Mr. Brickdale, seconded a motion rejecting it; one Liverpool merchant had reported that he had invested £30,000 in the slave trade and that a Bill like this would ruin him. The information about over-crowding and death that emerged from the debate on this issue gave added impetus to the Abolition movement. Bristol had one of the first provincial committees lobbying for total abolition of slavery; Joseph Harford was the Chairman, and Peter Lunell the Secretary.[8]

In June 1787, in Bristol, one of the first major blows in the campaign for abolition was delivered with the arrival in the city of the Rev. Thomas Clarkson, a leading opponent of slavery. Whilst a student, in 1784, he had written an essay (initially, an intellectual exercise) on the theme, 'Is it right to enslave men against their will ?'. He read one particular book, popular at the time, *Caution against the Slave Trade to Great Britain* by Anthony Benezet; his essay became a reasoned denunciation of the trade and the condition of slavery. He won a prize for the essay and began a crusade that would fight for abolition of the trade and emancipation of slaves.[9]

In 1786 Clarkson published his major work to date, *An Essay on the Slavery and Commerce of the Human Species, particularly to Africans*. He joined forces with another prominent Abolitionist, a solicitor, Richard Philips, and they set about gathering factual information about the slave trade. Rather than concentrate on the Africans, Clarkson decided to look at the lot of the British sailors on the Triangular route – this proved to be a valuable route for arousing public opinion.[10]

Clarkson might have failed to get his views made public and heard in the right quarter, had he not gained the active support of William Wilberforce, the M.P. for Yorkshire. Wilberforce was looking for a cause to carry forward his career and William Pitt, then the Prime Minister, suggested that he take up the case for abolition of the slave trade. Once he made his support known, Clarkson sent Wilberforce a copy of his Essay; a new and dynamic partnership had been formed.[11]

Clarkson set out on a journey around Britain that would last 5 months, visiting the towns and cities with direct interest in the slave trade. He wrote on approaching Bristol on 27 June 1787:

> '*The weather was rather hazy, which occasioned it to look of unusual dimensions ... It filled me, almost directly, with a melancholy for which I could not account. I began now to tremble for the first time at the arduous task I had undertaken, of attempting to subvert one of the branches of the commerce of the great place which was then before me... I anticipated much persecution in it also; and I questioned whether I should even get out of it alive ... When therefore I entered the city, I entered it with an undaunted spirit, determined that no labour should make me shrink, no danger, nor even persecution, deter me from my pursuit.*' [12]

His first step was to meet some of the city's abolitionists, the Quaker convert Harry

Goady (he had been a sailor on a slave ship before his crisis of conscience and conversion to Quakerism), James Harford, John Lury, Mathew Wright, Philip Debell Tuckett, Thomas Bonville and John Waring. Two clergymen met with Clarkson, the Rev. Dr. Camplin and Dean Tucker, who had written a pamphlet in 1785 castigating the slave trade for the number of murders that occurred as a result of its existence.[13] They were joined by Henry Sulgar, a Minister in the Moravian church, which also opposed the slave trade.[14]

In this same year, the Society for Effecting the Abolition of the Slave Trade was founded; amongst the earliest members were Granville Sharp, Thomas Clarkson, Richard Philips, William Wilberforce and the Rev. James Ramsay. It was Clarkson's idea that each area should form its own regional committee and that they should individually lobby Parliament in order to maximise the impact. An early member was Josiah Wedgwood who contributed the medallion designed by William Hackwood, one of his employees, that showed the kneeling slave in chains with the legend, 'Am I not a Man and a Brother?' In this early example of intensive marketing, Clarkson arranged for the image and slogan to appear on a variety of consumer goods – handkerchiefs, jewellery, china, snuff jars, medals, etc. – thereby bringing the message to a wide public audience.[15]

During their first year the members produced 51,432 books and pamphlets, 26,536 copies of reports and papers, and over 100 petitions to Parliament.[16] Many of the members of this national Society were, like many of the Bristol abolitionists, Quakers, a sect that had consistently opposed slavery. In Bristol the local Society were able to get a number of articles into the local press which in turn stimulated a campaign of letter writing, both for and against Abolition.

Not all religious bodies were against the slave trade. The Protestant churches of Bristol are full of examples of the baptisms, marriages and burials of slaves; there are even two examples from the records of the Catholic church of St. Mary on the Quay. In March 1793 was baptised *Josephus Athiops Africanus vulgo dictus Pope. Jos: cepit Thomas Donovan* (Joseph an Ethiopian of Africa, commonly called Joseph Pope, owned by Thomas Donovan) and in June 1789 *Baptizatus Johanne Franciscus Xavierus (vulgo dictus Jack Williams) Niger adultus ex Africa oriundus triginta quartuor circitor annorum aetatis. Susceperunt Nicolaus Duff et Catherina Watson.* [Baptism of John Francis Xavier (commonly called Jack Williams), an adult Negro from Africa, around 34 years old, sponsored by Nicholas Duff and Catherine Watson].[17]

However, the Quakers had been opposed to the trade almost since its beginning. As early as 1657 George Fox, the founder of the Society of Friends wrote, 'God…is no respecter of persons; but whosoever feareth him, and worketh righteousness, is accepted of Him. And He hath made all nations of one blood to dwell upon the face of the Earth.'[18] In 1671 at a Quaker meeting in Barbados George Fox called for all Friends to treat their slaves well and to free them 'after a considerable term of years'; they recognised that although slavery might be essential to agriculture, the slaves had rights as fellow men.[19] By the 1690s, Quakers in Pennsylvania confirmed that those who 'steal and rob men' and those who 'buy or purchase them, are they not all alike?'.[20]

In 1727 at the London Yearly Meeting, the Friends were warned against 'reaping the unrighteous profits arising from the iniquitous practice of dealing in slaves'. In 1775 they passed a ruling that **all** servants in Quaker households could become members of the Meeting House, provided they could produce a certificate of confirmation from their Quaker employer.[21] Quakers tried to disassociate themselves from the slave trade and in 1785 the Bristol and Frenchay Monthly Meeting Minutes recorded:

> 'We Friends are generally clear, not one person being engaged therein and holding anyone in slavery. Some few in the course of business furnish goods to merchants in that trade and only one family who from principle have retired from the West Indies to this city and have not yet been able to withdraw their properties, held mortgage on an estate wherein slaves are employed.'[22]

In 1785 the Quakers were responsible for distributing 300 copies of Anthony Benezet's book throughout the city.

The Methodists, one of Bristol's dissenting religious bodies, were also amongst the leading exponents of Abolition. As early as 1744 their leader, John Wesley, had written of the 'blood and guilt' of the Bristolians who engaged in the slave trade; the ship's captains who transported their captives, the merchants who arranged the voyages and the plantation owning gentlemen who fuelled the whole thing by their demand for labour. He advocated repentance and emancipation as the only Christian remedy:

> 'To the captains employed in this trade ... every merchant who is engaged in the slave-trade ... every gentleman that has an estate in our plantations ... Is there a God? You know there is. Is he a just God? Then there must be a state of retribution; a state wherein the just God will reward every man according to his works. Then what reward will He render you? O think betimes! Before you drop into eternity! Think now, 'He shall have judgement without mercy that showed no mercy'... Do you never feel another's pain? Have you no sympathy, no sense of human woe, no pity for the miserable? ... It is you that induce the African villain to sell his countrymen; and in order thereto, to steal, rob, murder men, women and children without number, by enabling the English villain to pay him for so doing, whom you overpay for his execrable labour. It is your money that is the spring of all, that empowers him to go on; so that whatever he or the African does in this matter is all your act and deed. And is your conscience quite reconciled to this?'.

When ... I entered the city, I entered it with an undaunted spirit, determined that no labour should make me shrink, no danger, nor even persecution, deter me from my pursuit', wrote Thomas Clarkson of his visit to Bristol in 1787. Thomas Clarkson after a painting by Samuel Lane, 1846. Wisbech & Fenland Museum

In 1788, as Wesley preached against the slave trade, a loud and violent noise assailed the Meeting House:

> *'The terror and confusion was inexpressible. The benches were broken in pieces, and nine-tenths of the congregation appeared to be struck with the same panic. In about six minutes the storm ceased. None can account for it without supposing some preternatural influence. Satan fought lest his kingdom should be delivered up.'* [23]

Unfortunately it was not so easy for American Methodists to stick to their guns over anti-slavery principles. In 1780 Methodist preachers in America were forbidden to buy slaves and in 1783 it was agreed that slaves already owned by ministers should be set free. The following year all Methodists were forbidden to trade in slaves and ordered to free any they did own within a year (or two, if they lived in a strong slave-owning state like Virginia). In 1785 however, these rules were relaxed as there had been a substantial exodus from the church by those unwilling to give up their slaves. In 1800 the rules for preachers were also relaxed and in 1804 the rules on buying and selling were quietly dropped. In fact by 1808 it was decided not to have any policy at all on the subject in America, leaving it to the moral judgement of each church member. Church leaders felt it was more important to keep their congregations and save their souls than insist on a policy that could not be upheld and alienated so many potential converts. Wesley cannot have been pleased at this softening of the moral position.[24]

Some members of Bristol's literary community also opposed slavery, often by means of their publications. Hannah More (1745-1833) spent most of her later life fighting for those she saw as needing her help. Apart from opposing slavery, she tried to help the Mendip miners and their families as well as agricultural workers, all of whom she saw as low-paid and disadvantaged. She offered spiritual, financial and educational help, publicising their cases in her work and through her many friends and contacts. She wrote poetry and plays and kept up correspondence with, amongst others, the politician and diarist Horace Walpole. On the subject of slavery, she was a fervent abolitionist. She wrote poems entitled *Slavery* and *The Sorrows of Yamba, or The Negro Woman's Lament*, the latter of which was published by the Newcastle Religious Tract Society.[25] I have already quoted from one of her letters to Walpole, who himself had written in 1750 about '...the British Senate, that temple of liberty, and bulwark of Protestant Christianity... pondering methods to make more effectual that horrid traffic of selling Negroes.'[26]

Daniel Defoe, famous for *Robinson Crusoe*, knew Bristol – indeed, legend had it that he met Alexander Selkirk, the model for Crusoe, in the *Llandogger Trow* Public House in King Street after his return to England from the desert island where he, Selkirk, had been marooned. In 1724 Defoe wrote *History of Pyrates* in which he expressed his revulsion to slavery and his belief that all men were equal.

The attitude of many Bristolians could be summed up in the verse written by an unknown contributor, published in the *Bristol Gazette* on 12 June 1788:

'I own I am shock'd at the purchase of slaves,
And fear those who buy them and sell them are knaves;
What I hear of their hardships, their tortures, and groans,
Is almost enough to drive pity from stones.
I pity them greatly, but I must be mum,
For how could we do without sugar and rum?
Especially sugar, so needful we see;
What, give up our dessert, our coffee and tea?'[27]

Clarkson was somewhat surprised to learn that most of the Bristolians he spoke to clearly recognised the abomination of the slave trade, particularly the brutality of the captains towards the sailors. Harry Goady, a Quaker and an ex-slave trader, told him, 'It was admitted on all hands that the captains and officers of the slave ships were noted for their brutality and that crews could be obtained only with extreme difficulty.'[28] He learned from Sydenham Teast, a leading ship builder, that a ship called the *Brothers* was currently still lying in port as no crew could be found. On her last voyage, 32 sailors had died, some as a direct result of the violence of the captain. One survivor, a Negro sailor called John Dean (a 'Negro' called John Dean was baptised at St Augustine the Less on 24 July 1761,[29] had been found guilty of some minor misdemeanour and the captain 'had fastened him to the deck, poured hot pitch upon his back, and made incisions in it with hot tongs'.[30]

Clarkson then learned of another ship, the *Alfred*, whose captain had also murdered at least one of his crewmen, but had been tried in Barbados and acquitted when he bribed the chief witness against him to disappear.[31] This captain had probably also caused the death of two other crew members and Clarkson thought a prosecution could be raised against him. However, he had a private conversation with Mr Burges, the deputy town clerk, who advised him against this course of action. Firstly, the judges would be merchants who always favoured the captains, whom they kept at their posts despite the accusations against them. Secondly, any witness from the crew would have to be financially supported while he remained in Bristol for many months before the trial occurred; and thirdly, the witness would probably be bribed by the merchants with a good berth on a ship to leave Bristol and effectively disappear.[32] Mr Burges gave it as his opinion that he 'only knew of one captain from the port in the slave trade who did not deserve long ago to be hanged'.[33]

Obviously Clarkson was intent upon presenting the captains of slaving ships in the worst possible light. In fact not all were violent thugs. Some rose to become agents, owners, investors and merchants. Some were businessmen who made substantial bonuses investing in voyages and were able to retire in a sound social and financial position. One example was John Fowler, Master of the *Molly* in 1750 and 1752; he went on to act as agent to 77 slaving voyages between 1758 and 1777.[34] In any debate on the question of slavery, Bristol was able to put forward at least one successful and respected ship's master to give evidence in its favour.[35]

Clarkson then set about looking at the methods used to get crews for the notorious slave ships. He headed for the city centre, to the area of seamen's lodging houses in King Street, Queen Street, Prince Street, Pipe Lane and Denmark Street. He visited a number of public houses where he observed 'music, dancing, rioting, and drunkenness, were kept up from night to night'. Some sailors were persuaded to sign on with the offer of enormous wages and bonuses; others were made hopelessly drunk so that they signed on without having any idea of what they were doing. A quicker method was to slip a drug into the drink so that the seaman could be taken on board without his agreement being needed. Another method was for the landlord to allow a sailor to run up a bill that he could not clear; he was then offered prison or the option of signing on with a slaver, so that an advance in his pay could be used to settle the debt. On many voyages, a sailor could expect to receive a month's money in advance; on a slaver he could receive two months' money, partly because of the length of time the trip was likely to take. Most experienced sailors knew the risks of the slavers – brutality, sickness and payment of wages in colonial currency, worthless outside the Indies.[36]

Clarkson was fortunate to meet Thompson, the landlord of the *Seven Stars* who disapproved of the slave trade and agreed to act as his guide around the drinking dens and who introduced him to crew members who could help him. His most valuable witnesses were found among the articulate professional men who served on ship. Amongst others, he interviewed Dr Gardiner, the surgeon on the *Pilgrim*, Alexander Falconbridge, surgeon on the *Alexander*, and his surgeon's mate, James Arnold. It was Falconbridge who told him about the seamen on the *Thomas* whose plight would lead to a court case.[37]

As a result of his investigations Clarkson found that he had sufficient evidence to bring a case against the Mate of the *Thomas* who had murdered one of the crew. The first hurdle was to present the case before a Bristol Bench – this consisted, in part, of several merchants, including one of the owners of the *Brothers* and *Alfred*. Clarkson recorded his feelings upon entering the court: 'I shall never forget the savage looks which the people (on the Bench) gave me, which indeed were so remarkable as to occasion the eyes of the whole court to be turned upon me.' Despite their attempts to have the case dismissed, the evidence was too strong and the Mate was sent to London for trial by the Admiralty Court. When the case was to be heard, Clarkson found that Burges had been right; two of the witnesses had been bribed and had disappeared off to sea; the other two had been forced to seek work in a Welsh colliery to support themselves during their wait. Clarkson went to Neath to find them and sent them to London. Luck was against him, as the case was heard only hours before his witnesses arrived and the Mate was found innocent through lack of evidence.[38]

Clarkson and the Bristol abolitionists did not have it all their own way. In 1789 a meeting was organised by the local West Indian plantation owners and merchants, held at the Merchants' Hall. Mr. William Miles presided over a meeting that aimed to defend the slave trade and the principle of slavery as it applied to Africans in the West Indies. Those who attended were amongst the wealthiest and most influential men of the city. They included Alderman Miles, Alderman Harris, Alderman Daubeny, Alderman Brice, Alderman Andrews (an ex-captain of a slave ship), Sir James Laroche, Thomas Daniel, Evan Bailie, John and William Gordon, Lowbridge and Richard Bright, John Fisher Weare, Robert Claxton, John Pinney, James Tobin, James Protheroe, Richard Vaughan, John Cave, James Morgan, James Harvey, Samuel Span, Henry and Robert Bush. Mr. Miles spoke on this occasion of the slave trade as being one 'on which the welfare of the West India islands and the commerce and revenue of the kingdom so essentially depend'.[39]

By this time, the opposition to the end of slave trading came almost exclusively from men such as these plantation owners and West Indian merchants; there were very few active slave traders left in the city. They briefed their MPs, Cruger and Brickdale, to speak on their behalf and began to assemble witnesses who would testify as to the benefits and advantages of the slave trade and the horrors that would attend its dismantling. The reasons for opposing abolition were many and varied. They included the point that if the trade stopped, the plantations would be unable to find a work force and would have to cease farming. Other countries would move in, take the land and use it to harvest crops and supply bases for their naval forces, thereby diminishing Britain's naval supremacy. It was argued that Africans would suffer if they were denied trade with England, that compensation in vast amounts would have to be paid just at the time when trade and the revenue from it were reduced. They argued that Bristol in particular would become a ruined wasteland with most of its inhabitants, who were involved in some way with the African or West Indian trade, brought to total ruin. It was said that Bristol's sugar refineries would cease to function as old plantations fell into disuse and new ones failed to be cultivated:

> 'Any check to the ample supply of this article [African slaves] would not only be ruinous in the extreme to the petitioners engaged in the manufacture [of sugar] but the mischief would extend most widely, throwing many hundreds of common labouring people...wholly out of employment...the cultivation of the West India colonies cannot be carried on...the decline of the trade of the City of Bristol must inevitably follow.'[40]

Other arguments were that the debts of the planters would have to be written off, causing bankruptcies amongst Bristol's merchants and the Newfoundland fisheries would fail as their trade with the West Indies to supply fish for feeding slaves was reduced to nothing. In any case, it was said, slaves were better off than English people in prisons or indeed than many of the labouring classes in mills, mines and factories.

When William Wilberforce moved Acts in Parliament to curtail and abolish the slave trade, Mr. Cruger, Bristol's MP (Mathew Brickdale, the other, being ill), answered on behalf of the Bristol Corporation and merchant community. He presented six petitions, from the African Committee, the West Indies merchants, Bristol manufacturers, the Corporation, the Merchant Venturers and the Newfoundland Merchants. It was obvious from his response that the merchants were not averse to abandoning the trade in slaves that was becoming so difficult and yielding smaller profits. He suggested that the trade could be regulated and eventually abolition could be gradually achieved; however, if it were to be attempted quickly, the injured owners would require £60-70 million in compensation. Abolition was not agreed but the Bill of 1788 was confirmed and strengthened. From this time, Bristol's involvement in the slave trade began its final decline in earnest.[41]

The problem was that a significant number of MPs were either merchants who had grown wealthy through their part in the slave trade or who had an interest in plantations that still relied on slave labour. They would be extraordinarily difficult for the sincere abolitionists to out-vote.

The battle lines were joined in Parliament from this time forward. In February 1788 the first of a number of investigations was started under the aegis of the Trade and Plantation Committee, whose remit was to enquire into commerce with Africa, including the slave trade. Clarkson and Philips were able to use the information they had marshalled to present the case for Abolition. Their mass of information was seen as stronger than the large number of witnesses who were presented by those who favoured retaining the slave trade, at least for the present, and the state of slavery for as long as it was economically necessary.

Africans in England also spoke out during the enquiries. During the debate on the rights and wrongs of slavery, Prince John Henry Naimbanna, son of King Naimbanna of Sierra Leone, made a speech on behalf of Africans:

> *'If a man should try to kill me, or should sell my family for slaves, he would do an injury to as many as he might kill or sell, but if any one takes away the character of a black people, there is nothing which he may not do to black people ever after. That man for instance, will beat black men, and say 'O, it is only a black man, why should I not beat him'. That man will make slaves of black people; for when he has taken away their character, he will say, 'O, they are only black people, why should I not make them slaves?' That man will take away all the people of Africa, if he can catch them, and if you ask him, 'Why do you take away all those people', he will say, 'O, they are only black people, they are not like white people, why should not I take them?' That is the reason I cannot forgive the man who takes away the character of the people of my country.'* [42]

Amongst the pro-slavery witnesses sent by the Bristol merchants was James

Tobin, a plantation owner from Nevis. He had had previous dealings with one of the city's leading abolitionists, James Ramsay, the Anglican clergyman who had gained practical experience of the state of slavery during his time on St. Kitts. Ramsay said of those he knew who bought and sold slaves, as well as those who owned them, 'they had never examined the nature of this commerce and went into it, and acted as others had done before them in it, as a thing of course, for which no account was to be given in this world or the next'. The two men engaged in a pamphlet 'war' in 1784. Tobin's argument for maintaining the trade seemed to be that the plantations needed a work force – and that every European country was doing it:

> *'It has indeed ever been my opinion that neither the slavery of the West India colonies, or the commerce of the human species, are to be defended, except on political grounds, and the general practice of all the most enlightened nations'.*[43]

The feeling amongst many of the anti-abolitionists was that 'a limited evil must be tolerated in order to sustain a general prosperity'.[44]

Amongst other pro-slavery 'expert' witnesses were Governor Parry and Mr. Brathwaite, an Agent for the Assembly, both from Barbados. They were asked a series of questions and described the life of a slave. They discussed the slave's regular diet (Guinea or Indian corn, plantains, potatoes, yams, maize, rice and salt-fish) and the additional food that could be produced on a piece of land that the slave was allowed to use to raise their own supplemental diet. Indeed, Governor Parry reported, 'Upon the whole, the general condition of slaves in this Island may be said to be better than that of a poor White Inhabitant.' They admitted that there were no laws, as such, to provide adequate food, clothing, housing or medical assistance but suggested that this was provided anyway, without recourse to law, by sensible and concerned owners. They reported that slaves tended to live as long as white people but that the women tended to produce fewer children (which necessitated the maintenance of the slave trade with Africa). They were both at a loss to explain this, suggesting that it could be due to a general promiscuity, drink and disease amongst the female slaves, the 'carelessness' of the mothers, hurricanes – and just possibly, in some very few cases, over-work. No mention was made of floggings and beatings of pregnant women working in the fields in their seventh or eighth month of pregnancy or of the trauma of previous children having been sold away from their parents.[45]

In the event, the first Enquiry culminated in the introduction of Sir William Dolben's Bill to regulate the conditions on board slave ships and set a minimum space for each slave during transportation:

> *'... after the 10th June, 1788, it shall not be lawful for any master, or any other person taking the charge or command of any ship or vessel whatever, belonging in the whole or in part to any port in this kingdom, to*

have on board, at any one time, or to convey or transport the natives of Africa from the coast thereof, to any island in the West Indies, belonging to His Majesty, or to any other place in parts beyond sea, in any greater number than in the proportions following: In every ship, where the space between the two decks shall not be less than five feet in height, and where the cabin shall be fitted for the accommodation of the Negroes, in the proportions of five persons to three tons, if the burden of the ship does not exceed 160 tons; and of three persons for two tons, if the burden of the ship does not exceed 150 tons; and in every ship where the space between the two decks shall be less than five feet, or where the cabin shall not be fitted for the accommodation of Negroes, in the proportion of one person for every ton burden of the ship or vessel in or on board which such natives shall be so conveyed, carried, brought or transported, as aforesaid; which tonnage shall be deemed and taken to be the tonnage described and set forth in the respective certificate of the registry of each ship or vessel, granted in pursuance of an act made in the 26th year of the reign of His Majesty ... under the penalty of the forfeiture of £20 for every native exceeding in number the proportion directed.' [46]

It was a telling point that even with the provisions of the Bill, convicted criminals being transported got twice the space allowed for a slave.

This relatively mild Bill raised arguments such as the one involving James Jones of Bristol who had nine ships running slaves; if he were obliged to give each the proposed space, he would lose one quarter of his cargo and face stark ruin as a result. He gave evidence that if a merchant sending out a ship of 200 tons:

'...does not purchase 400 slaves, and more, she must certainly sink the Owner's Money — because the mere Expense of Carriage of that Number amounts to near Nine Pounds per Head; consequently, every Slave she carries less, she loses so many Nine Pounds.' [47]

Despite this kind of point, in July 1788 Dolben's Bill became law and the first blow was struck for the legal abolition of the slave trade. In April 1789 Clarkson followed this up by issuing a print of diagrams for packing the Liverpool ship the *Brookes* with 482 slaves. It cold-bloodedly showed the outlines of men, women and children, packed like sardines, lying shoulder to shoulder and head to toe, covering every inch of the space below decks without any room to move. The image was powerful and its impact immediate; it became known as *The Print*, was widely circulated and kept the question of the slave trade alive and potent.[48]

In 1789 the Privy Council published an 850-page report of their findings, which produced a summary of the evidence but reached no conclusions. Clarkson used the report to produce a speech for Wilberforce that he gave during a debate. His

Anti-slavery activist Thomas Clarkson was fortunate to meet Thompson, the landlord of the Seven Stars. Thompson introduced Clarkson to crew members who could supply evidence to support the abolitionist's cause. The Seven Stars Public House, Thomas Lane, Bristol. (M.Manson)

speech lasted three and a half hours and signalled his place as the leading spokesman for the Abolition movement. He wanted a vote taken on the question but again the pro-slavery lobby arranged for a request to be passed for another enquiry.[49] One reason for the delay was a fear of France; that if Britain ceased to trade in slaves and the demand remained, the French would fill the gap by picking up the trade Britain had relinquished. Bristol certainly was trading slaves, not only with the English-controlled islands in the West Indies but with Dutch St. Eustasius, Spanish Cuba and Puerto Rico and French Guadeloupe and Martinique. France, too, had an Abolition movement but each country was waiting for the other to make the first move; it did not help that war was already looming with France.

In January 1790 the Government convened a Select Committee to study the question of the slave trade. The first witness called was a Bristol captain, James Fraser, who had commanded a slave ship – rumour had it that he was selected by the Bristol merchants as he was the only respectable captain in the entire city! One of Fraser's replies, to the question of the low pay of the sailors on board Guineamen, was that they were often 'half-trained' novices and would not receive the pay of real sailors. It was noticeable that no captain was called to represent Liverpool.[50]

Bristol, meanwhile, had elected two new MPs, the Marquis of Worcester, heir of the Duke of Beaufort (who never spoke in Parliament) and John Baker Holroyd, Lord Sheffield, who became the city's pro-slavery spokesman. He admitted that the trade was cruel, that there should be reform, that both slaves and sailors should be better treated, that plantations should implement a kinder regime and that the volume of slave trading should be reduced. However, he argued that as all European countries could not agree on Abolition, Britain could not go it alone, and that the existing slaves should not be suddenly freed, as they were like helpless children without the wise guidance of the white colonists.[51]

Clarkson, as before, assembled a number of witnesses, among them Isaac Parker, who had actually been on a slaving raid. Normally, the Bristol ships would arrive and wait on the Coast for slaves, already brought from the interior, to be loaded by boat or canoe from the forts and trading settlements. Parker, however, described how he and other crew members had been invited to take part in a raiding party, how they had attacked a village and kidnapped the local people:

> 'They [the slave traders] then concealed themselves under the bushes, which hung over the water from the banks. In this position they remained during day-light. But at night they went up to it armed and seized all the inhabitants who had not time to make their escape ... They seized men, women and children, as they could find them in the huts.'

The natives were then tied up and brought down river by canoe to be loaded on to his ship for transportation.[52]

Clarkson found it very difficult to get his witnesses, even for matters that were common knowledge. Most of them were people who had been actively involved in the trade; some were afraid of retribution, some were fearful of losing their livelihood. Some had joined the slave trade because they were unfit for any other (possibly because they were drug addicts, alcoholics or mentally ill) and so made unreliable witnesses under cross-examination. Some merely wanted to wait and see which side of the abolition argument was going to win in order to decide where they would bestow their support. Another problem for Clarkson was that he was seen as being pro-French, given his support for the French Abolition movement and his open admiration for the French Revolution made him a dangerous radical in many political eyes.

A willing witness who addressed the Committee was Olaudah Equiano (also called Gustavus Vassa, a name given him by one of his masters while he was a slave). He had published his book, *The Interesting Narrative of the Life of Olaudah Equiano or Gustavus Vassa, the African, written by Himself,* the year before and he was asked to speak as an expert witness on the situation in Africa. Apart from being an advocate of Abolition, he also supported fair trade with Africa.

The Select Committee reported in April 1791 and Wilberforce moved a Bill for Abolition of the Slave Trade; it was defeated, 163 votes to 88.[53]

Notes
1   Gifford, Zerbanoo, *Thomas Clarkson and the Campaign Against Slavery* (1996), p.8-9
2   Sherwood, Marika, *Black Peoples in the Americas* (1992), p.35-6
3   Gifford, Zerbanoo, op cit, p.9-10
4   ibid p.10-1]
5   Latimer, John, *Annals of Bristol in the Eighteenth Century* (1970), p.49
6   Robinson, Derek, *A Shocking History of Bristol* (1973), p.61-4
7   Richardson, David, (ed), *Bristol, Africa and the 18th Century Slave Trade to America: The Years of Decline 1746-68*, Vol.3 (1991), p.85
8   Latimer, John, *The History of the Society of Merchant Venturers of the City of Bristol* (1903), p.185
9   Gifford, Zerbanoo, op cit, p.7
10 ibid p19
11 ibid p.21
12 Ballard, Martin, Bristol Sea-Port City (1966), p.85
13 Latimer, John, The Annals of Bristol in the Eighteenth Century (1970), p.473
14 Marshall, Peter, 'The Anti-Slave Trade Movement in Bristol, McGrath, Patrick (ed.), *Bristol in the Eighteenth Century* (1972), p.188
15 Dresser, Madge & Giles, Sue, *Bristol and Transatlantic Slavery* (1999), p.82-3
16 Gifford, Zerbanoo, op cit, p.25
17 Lindegaard, DP, *Bristol Roots: Black Bristolians in the 17th, 18th and 19th Centuries* (1990), p.33, 45
18 Craton, Michael, Walvin, James, Wright, David, Slavery, Abolition and Emancipation (1976), p.202
19 Sherwood, Marika, Black Peoples in the Americas (1992), p.32
20 Everett, Susanne, History of Slavery (1997), p.134
21 pers. com. Anya Summers
22 Marshall, Peter, op cit, p.187
23 John Wesley, *Thoughts upon Slavery*, 1774, reprinted by the John Wesley Chapel
24 McColley, Robert, *Slavery and Jeffersonian Virginia* (1964), p.152
25 Hannah More, *The Sorrows of Yamba, Edward Walter, Pilgrim Street, Newcastle for the Newcastle Religious Society*
26 Williams, Eric, Capitalism and Slavery (1975), p.41
27 Dresser, Madge & Giles, Sue, op cit, p.54
28 Latimer, John, op cit, p.474
29 Bristol Record Office, FCP/StAug/R/1
30 Pope-Hennessy, James, Sins of the Fathers, (1967), p.257
31 Latimer, John, op cit, p.474
32 Marshall, Peter, op cit, p.189
33 ibid, p.189
34 Richardson, David, The Bristol Slave Traders: A Collective Portrait (1985), p.29
35 Marshall, Peter, op cit, p.203
36 Latimer, John, op cit, p.475
37 Marshall, Peter, op cit, p.190-1
38 Latimer, John, op cit, p.476
39 ibid p.476-7
40 Robinson, Derek, op cit, p.70
41 Latimer, John, op cit, p.477
42 Gifford, Zerbanoo, op cit, p.26
43 Marshall, Peter, op cit, p.196
44 ibid p.199
45 Craton, Michael, Walvin, James, & Wright, David, *Slavery, Abolition and Emancipation* (1976), p.87-97
46 Craton, Michael, Walvin, op cit, p.87-97
47 Richardson, David, (ed), *Bristol, Africa and the 18th Century Slave Trade to America: The Final Years 1770-1807*, Vol.4 (1991), p.xxxi
48 Gifford, Zerbanoo, op cit, p.28
49 ibid, p.28
50 Marshall, Peter, op cit, p.203-4
51 ibid p.205
52 Ballard, Martin, op cit, p.86
53 Gifford, Zerbanoo, op cit, 34

TWELVE

MERCHANTS AT HOME & WEALTHY

The merchants who flourished despite the problems with the American, African and West Indian Trade in the second half of the 18th century, usually moved into other areas of trade and took their place in the upper classes. When James Sketchely produced the first *Bristol Directory* in 1775, it was a book that largely ignored the working classes and provided: 'An Alphabetical list of the Merchants, Tradesmen, Manufacturers, Captains of Ships, Custom House and Excise Officers, and every other person of note in Bristol and its environs'.

John Aitkin, writing in 1788, detailed some of the trades that made Bristol wealthy in these years:

> *'The glass-making, in its several articles of crown, flint, and bottle glass, is very considerable and on the increase. Ireland and America (now independent) take off great quantities of these goods, especially bottles, of which nearly half the number are sent out filled with beer, cyder, perry, and Bristol water. The copper and brass manufacturers were of capital importance, but are now much declined in consequence of a monopoly. Hard white soap, of the best quality, is made here in large quantities, much of which is sent to London, as well as to the colonies abroad. Hats, leather, both tanned and dressed in oil, saddlery and shoes, white lead, gunpowder and earthen-ware, are all considerable articles of domestic and foreign traffic. The city likewise possesses works for smelting lead and making lead shot, iron foundries, rolling and slitting mills, and the tin works, all of which furnish very valuable commodities for exportation. Its former woollen manufactures are at an end.'*

Aitkin then goes on to list some of the commodities that are brought into Bristol for re-export:

> *'... cheese, cyder, and beer, a few coals, herrings taken in the channel, salt from Droitwich, coarse woollens and stockings, hardware from Birmingham and Wolverhampton, and earthenware from Staffordshire.'*[1]

An article in the *Gentleman's Magazine* of 1799 quoted the range of Bristol's trade partners:

> '*The Merchants of Bristol enjoy the trade of Ireland, and of nearly the whole of North and South Wales. In exchanging commodities with the West Indies, they employ no less than seventy ships, and this is one of the most important branches of their commerce. They also traffic with Spain, Portugal, Guinea, Holland, Hamburgh, Norway, Russia, America, and Newfoundland.*'[2]

Aitkin also noted that Liverpool was fast over-hauling Bristol in many areas of trade; however he concluded:

> '*Bristol, in wealth, trade, and population, has long been reckoned second to London within this Kingdom; and though the custom house receipts of Liverpool have for some time past exceeded those of Bristol, yet the latter may perhaps still maintain its place with respect to the opulence and number of its inhabitants.*'[3]

The upper classes in Bristol still had their Negro servants; church records, broadsheets and newspapers carried references to births, marriages, deaths, and outstanding events. In the 1740s, two marriages are recorded between African men and Bristol women – John Gloucester married Mary Ven in 1746, and in the following year, John Williams married Ruth Fitzgerald.[4]

As to the news, court cases, then as now, proved of interest; in 1749, recorded in the *Bristol Weekly Intelligencer*, a Negro, William Jones was committed for trial before Alderman Jacob Elton, 'he being charged on oath with having threatened the life of Mathew Craven, Master of the ship, *Peggy*'. Why, one wonders? A rather more specific case was heard in 1771 and reported in *Sarah Farley's Bristol Journal*, when two Negroes, John Tillaboo and Hampshire, were jointly charged with Hugh Hanford, a labourer, with the theft of 9 hundredweight of wet sugar. In the event, Hampshire and Hanford were acquitted, but Tillaboo was transported for 7 years.

A few of the slaves had managed to preserve elements of their African origins in their names – John Tillaboo was one, as were John Ancoo, Mingo, John Gambo, John Saggee and Sarah Baribo.[5]

Of more financial interest to the reader was the steady stream of advertisements for slaves who had 'eloped' and the reward offered for their return. They throw an interesting light on the costume of the African in Bristol, giving the clothes in which each man was last seen. Two examples were published in *Felix Farley's Journal*. In 1746 Mingo, the slave of Captain Thomas Eaton of the ship *Prince William*, eloped wearing 'a black wig, had on two short blue waistcoats, and brown breeches'. In 1754 it was the turn of John Lopes Constant, owned by John Young of Redcliffe Hill, dressed in 'a blue-grey coat and white Holland waistcoat, a pair of black cloth breeches, a lorified cap, and a pair of light coloured worsted stockings'.

The other great staple of the news, show business, also featured a Negro performer. In *Felix Farley's Journal* for 4 June 1752:

> 'We are assured that the African Prince, or Surprising Negro, and the famous new Chien Savant, or learned Dog, will be exhibited both together at our next ensuing St. James Fair a the Three Tons on St. James Back. The said Negro in a most accountable manner brings his hands flat clasp'd over his head, back and under his legs and this he does backwards as well as forwards without ever disengaging them. He likewise does several new and astonishing performances on the slack-wire and has had the honour to be seen by the Royal Society at their general Meeting in December last in Crane Court, Fleet Street, London, with universal admiration.'

Notes
1   Marcy, Peter T, *'Eighteenth Century Views of Bristol and Bristolians'*, McGrath, Patrick (ed.), Bristol in the Eighteenth Century (1972), p.15]
2   Marcy, Peter T, op cit, p.18
3   ibid p.3
4   Lindegaard, DP, *Bristol Roots: Black Bristolians in the 17th, 18th and 19th Centuries* (1990), p.22, 45
5   Lindegaard, DP, op cit, p.42

THIRTEEN

In 1789 the result of the Royal Commission on Slavery was published. They had spent more than a year taking evidence from a range of those who supported and opposed slavery. Their findings made damning reading. The Report was set out under six headings; the first concerned the state of the Guinea Coast and the countries that provided slaves. For the merchants and planters, Captain Thomas Deane of Bristol gave evidence on the acquiring of slaves and John Anderson of the Merchant Venturers spoke on how efficiently the trade was carried out. Clarkson's evidence to the contrary was then presented and supplemented by a statement from James Arnold, surgeon on board the *Ruby* under Captain Joseph Williams, whom he characterised as a vicious tyrant, bully and cheat.

The second heading, the Middle Passage and treatment of the slaves, again saw Arnold give evidence concerning his voyages, including the latest one on the *Ruby*. He said that the crewmen were treated almost as badly as the slaves, suffering bad food, cramped and unsanitary conditions and floggings at the whim of the captain. The fourth heading concerned the extent of the slave trade. Despite Bristol's constant assertions that the city would face ruin if the slave trade were abolished, figures presented suggested that African trade, slaves as well as gold, ivory, spices and wood, accounted for only 30 ships of the city's overseas trade – hardly the major source of revenue suggested previously. The abolitionists were anxious to see the trade with Africa separated from the trade with the West Indies; if the two were added together, then the number rose to 109 out of a total of 221 – almost half. The link was, of course, made by the pro-slavery lobby, which saw abolition of the trade and eventual emancipation as the death knell for Caribbean trade in general.[1] In 1787, 44 ships arrived in Bristol from North America and 76 from the West Indies, with only 15 from Africa; 185 came from Europe and 163 from Ireland.[2]

The French Revolution broke out in 1789 and for some years the Government became highly suspicious of anything that referred to Liberty, Equality and Fraternity – which put 'Am I Not a Man and a Brother?' and indeed the whole anti-slavery campaign, in a dubious political light, especially as some of the foremost champions of the movement were also supporters of the ideals of the French Revolution. Anyone advocating abolition could be seen as potentially offering the French the entire, and still lucrative, slave trade. The French did not help matters by opening their markets in the West Indies to the Americans, and by using American ports for refitting and revictualling.[3] A relationship arose between France and America, fuelled by the French offering access to European markets, especially for tobacco, that bypassed the hated British. On top of that the French forged a political alliance, agreeing to help the Americans against the Spanish who still held control of Louisiana and Florida.

The newly-formed United States of America formally abolished the slave trade in the northern states but despite mounting feeling against it, slavery still flourished in the southern states. One driving factor had been the invention by Eli Whitney of the Cotton Gin in 1793 that revolutionised cotton production. This machine separated cotton fibre from seed. If this work were done by hand, it was calculated that one man could deal with 1lb in a day; one man operating a gin could treat 50lbs. This meant economic boom for the south, but only if it had the (slave) workforce. In 1808 the American Congress banned the slave trade but slaves were still smuggled in, usually via purchases made in Brazil and Cuba. Obadiah Brown wrote in a letter about Bristol, Rhode Island:

> *'The impunity with which prohibited traffic is carried on from this Place has for some time past rendered it the resort of many violators of common law … The African slave trade is the one of this description now most successfully and extensively prosecuted.'*[4]

In 1891 Congress declared all slave traders to be the equivalent of pirates and trading to be punishable by the death penalty. Any slaves found on board a seized ship were liberated and returned to Africa, the rescue funded by Congress. The US also founded an African state for these freed slaves and for any slaves in America who wanted to return to their homeland, called Liberia. The capital city was named Monrovia, in honour of President Monroe who was a strong supporter of this scheme.[5]

In Bristol in 1790, Messrs. Cruger and Brickdale having stood down, two new MPs were elected, the Marquis of Worcester and Lord Sheffield, the latter being an advocate of the continuation of the slave trade whose many supporters had strong West Indian connections. Sheffield spoke in favour of the continuation of the slave trade whenever the question arose and wrote Observations on the Project for Abolishing the Slave Trade in 1790. He argued that although there had been instances of cruelty to both slaves and sailors, what was needed was parliamentary regulation both in England and in the West Indies, to better the lot of both groups. He also suggested that taxes and compensation payments could reduce the number of slaves, and those in the West Indies could gradually achieve a form of life-long 'apprenticeship' whereby they would be technically free but still bound to serve a particular master. Although Sheffield was a Whig, he gained the wholehearted support of the Tory Bristol merchants since he supported them on this subject.[6]

In 1791, during a debate on abolition of the slave trade, Lord Sheffield stated that the views of the abolitionist were purely hysterical; he even doubted that Parliament had the right to ban the selling of slaves. Wilberforce presented his evidence again, but Sheffield and his supporters triumphed. His opinion was supported with 163 votes against 88.[7]

Clarkson, however, was trying a different tack. His organisation promoted a national sugar boycott which it was hoped would have a positive influence on the West Indian planters, if they saw their sales affected. He estimated about 300,000 families had agreed to the ban – in Bristol it was supported by the Bristol and Clifton Auxiliary Ladies Anti-Slavery Society (ladies of the Goldney family were members).[8]

Women might not have the vote but Clarkson saw them, quite rightly, as having a major domestic impact on the votes cast by the men.

However, that same year, another atrocity took place. Six merchant ships, including the *Thomas*, *Wasp* and *Recovery* from Bristol, threatened to bombard the town of Calabar – they thought the traders were asking too high a price for slaves. In the event, no reply was received and the ships opened fire on the town, shelling it for several hours until the natives submitted.[9] In April 1792 William Wilberforce, during a debate on abolition, reported the attack in the House of Commons, how 20 Negroes were killed and many more wounded, just so that merchants from Liverpool and Bristol could make a few extra pounds. At the time, slaves cost £22 in Africa but were fetching £40-50 in the West Indies.[10]

Wilberforce was particularly disgusted that the captains of the ships had been welcomed back by their employers and given further commands. One of them, Captain John Kimber, Master of the *Recovery*, was taken to Court to answer the charges relating to the attack on Calabar. Captain Kimber was also accused of torturing and killing a 15-year-old African girl, a slave being taken on the Middle Passage. In the event, the chief prosecution witnesses, William Dowling, the surgeon and Stephen Devereux, a seaman, were the only ones who spoke out against Kimber; on his behalf, one of the owners of the *Recovery*, Walter Jacks, gave Kimber a glowing character. On the question of the attack on Calabar, his version (that the bombardment had caused no loss of life) was supported by Thomas Phillips, the Captain of the *Thomas*. The surgeon on this ship reported that Dowling had an animus against Kimber, and the second mate of the *Wasp* also appeared to confirm the reports of the others present at Calabar on the occasion of the bombardment. Kimber further testified that the slave girl in question had died of disease, not ill-treatment. In the light of the lack of overwhelming evidence, Kimber was acquitted but the case had already been widely publicised and this became a *cause celebre* and a powerful weapon in the abolition movement.

In 1792 the House of Commons met again to debate a motion to abolish the slave trade. At 6.00 p.m., Wilberforce rose to open the debate, and the speakers carried on, ending with the Prime Minister, William Pitt, who finished at 6.00 a.m. the following morning. A suggested amendment was that abolition should take place gradually, 'in moderation'. An exasperated Charles James Fox replied, 'How can you carry on the slave trade moderately? How can a country be pillaged and destroyed in moderation? We cannot modify injustice.'[12] However, the pro-slavery members would not vote for total abolition and agreed to support the amendment; the abolitionists felt that moderation was better than another defeat. It was agreed that the slave trade should be abolished gradually, starting in January 1796, but the House of Lords moved that

William Wilberforce MP by George Richmond, 1833. (National Portrait Gallery) His speech to Parliament lasted 3.5 hours, and signalled his place as the leading spokesman for the Abolition movement.

all the evidence for and against the slave trade should be heard yet again! As it turned out, neither move was ever implemented, as war with France intervened.

In February 1793 war was declared between England and France, on the occasion of the execution of King Louis XVI. In Bristol, chaos reigned; for many years, the local banks had been lending money and encouraging speculation and now, with war declared, about 100 provincial banks stopped payments for a few days. In the event, all bank-notes were honoured, but credit was tightened and some of the larger speculators were made bankrupt[13] – one of the more prominent was Walter Jacks, the erstwhile co-owner of the infamous *Recovery*.[14] Many of the Bristol bankers were, or had been, involved in the slave trade and they had to be far more careful with their money for a while. A number of building projects, like those in Clifton and Kingsdown, were halted, leaving half-completed, roofless houses from Portland Square to Royal York Crescent.[15]

With so many leading merchants in financial difficulties and the threat of French privateers, not surprisingly the slave trading voyages dropped off. Even Matthew's *Directory* for 1793-4 noted, 'the ardour for trade to Africa for men and women, our fellow creatures and equals, is much abated among the humane and benevolent merchants of Bristol'.[16] In the House of Lords, however, the Duke of Clarence who had served with the Royal Navy in the Caribbean, was reporting on having seen slaves living in 'humble happiness';[17] his Royal Highness also described abolitionists as 'either fanatics or hypocrites', adding, 'and in one of these classes I rank Mr Wilberforce,' a statement so ridiculous that it created an uproar.[18]

In April 1794 the French-controlled West Indian island of Martinique fell to the British. In May, Guadeloupe was taken and in July, Port au Prince. France had gone to the lengths of abolishing slavery in the hope that the freed slaves would fight for France against the English in the Caribbean – as the English took each island, they reinstated the state of slavery. This gave Britain control of the main French colonies (all of whom needed to be supplied with slaves) and in common with other cities, Bristol was illuminated in celebration – John Weekes, landlord of the *Bush Inn*, served free drinks.[19] This jubilation was tempered by the bad harvests of 1794 and 1795 that led to serious shortages of bread, and food riots. In the early years of the 1800s, this problem was compounded by the closure of most European ports to English shipping, thanks to Napoleon having once more declared war, which severely curtailed imports of grain. With all this, the cause of abolition and emancipation tended to lose its impact.

In 1795, in response to the French War, the Government passed a law that suspended all merchant shipping until each city supplied a fixed number of sailors for the Royal Navy, always an unpopular berth with seamen. London was asked to find 5,704 men, Liverpool, 1,240, and Bristol 666, fewer than Hull or Sunderland. Bristol got her quota together by May, half being experienced seamen and half 'landsmen', that is, not trained sailors.[20] The war had hit Bristol's trading fleet badly. In 1792, 480 ships paid the Mayor's Dues; in 1796, it fell to 304.[21] In that same year, the Royal

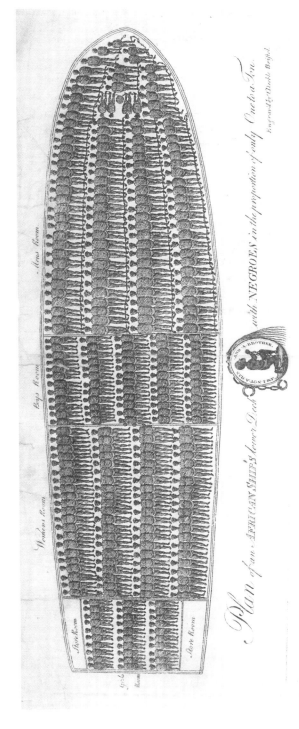

Plan of an AFRICAN SHIP'S lower Deck with NEGROES in the proportion of only One to a Tone.

Engraved & Sold by Deeble Bristol.

Published by the Plymouth Committee of Abolitionists, 1788, from an engraving by Deeble, Bristol. Shows the Liverpool ship the Brookes packed with 482 slaves. It became known as 'The Print' and was widely circulated by abolitionists. (Bristol Record Office)

Navy organised a convoy of 100 ships to the West Indies; 66 came from London, 28 from Liverpool, and only 6 from Bristol. In 1797, of 144 ships leaving Jamaica for England, only 17 came to Bristol; the following year it was 16 out of 150. As a result, the amount of sugar entering the city for refining fell dramatically and in 1800 Bristol had to import sugar through Liverpool.[22]

Sugar refining was a major industry in Bristol. By 1799 there were 20 refineries in the city, which benefited from cheap West Indian raw material and a good supply of local coal. Despite abolition of the slave trade, in 1811 the number of refineries had dropped by only 4 but it was not until the end of the 19th century that sugar refining in Bristol ended altogether.[23]

A truce was signed with France in October 1801 and peace declared in May 1802. This peace, however, was short-lived, and War broke out again in the summer of 1803. It was not until June 1814 that a final peace was declared and Bristol was once more en fete. Further cause for rejoicing came in the spring of 1815 when, with the Treaty of Ghent, the war with America came to an end. In 1802, however, the question of abolition was once again brought to the fore and it became obvious that there was massive public support for it. To this end, even the West Indian merchants and planters tempered their opposition, recognising the hopelessness of their situation. All they could hope for now was to keep the question of emancipation out of the issue.

In 1805 a Bill abolishing the slave trade was passed by the House of Commons but foundered in the House of Lords; the following year the Bill was presented again and failed by only 7 votes – it later transpired that 9 anti-slavery MPs had been absent on the day. With their support, and that of the Irish MPs who had no vested interest in the slave trade and who had also been unable to attend, Clarkson and Wilberforce were confident that they could carry the Bill in the next session. Sadly, William Pitt, the Prime Minister, died but fortunately he was replaced by another anti-slavery Minister, Lord Grenville; his Foreign Secretary was Charles James Fox, another staunch abolitionist.[24]

Notes

1   Marshall, Peter, *The Anti-Slave Trade Movement in Bristol*, McGarth, Patrick (ed.), *Bristol in the Eighteenth Century* (1972), p.197-9
2   Douglas, Professor David, Ralph, Elizabeth, *The Trade of Bristol on the Eighteenth Century* (1966), p.181
3   McColey, Robert, Slavery and Jeffersonian Virginia (1964), p.51
4   Duigan, Peter & Clendenen, Clarence, *The United States and the African Slave Trade 1619-1862* (1963), p.18-9
5   Duigan, Peter & Clendenen, Clarence, op cit, p.21-3
6   Marshall, Peter, op cit, p.205
7   Latimer, John, *The Annals of Bristol in the Eighteenth Century* (1970), p.477
8   Bristol Central Library, Local History - Estling Archive
9   Latimer, John, *The History of the Society of Merchant Venturers of the City of Bristol* (1903), p.186
10 Latimer, John, The Annals of Bristol in the Eighteenth Century (1970), p.477-8
11 Marshall, Peter, op cit, p.206-8
12 Gifford, Zerbanoo, *Thomas Clarkson and the Campaign Against Slavery* (1996), p.38
13 Latimer, John, *The Annals of Bristol on the Eighteenth Century* (1970), p.499-500
14 Marshall, Peter, op cit, p.213
15 Latimer, John, *The Annals of Bristol in the Eighteenth Century* (1970), p.494-5
16 Marshall, Peter, op cit, p.211
17 Gifford, Zerbanoo, op cit, 40
18 Fulford, Roger, *Royal Dukes: Queen Victoria's 'Wicked Uncles'* (1933), p.107
19 Latimer, John, op cit, p.506
20 ibid p.514
21 ibid p.517
22 ibid p.519
23 Williams, Eric, *Capitalism and Slavery* (1975), p.74
24 Gifford, Zerbanoo, op cit, p.44-5

FOURTEEN

In 1806, Parliament passed a law forbidding the trade in slaves between Africa and the recently acquired West Indian colonies. There were also bills condemning the slave trade in principle, banning the commissioning of new ships into the trade and requesting the King, George III, to press other European heads of state to abolish the slave trade. This was seen as essential, as one of the most powerful fears holding up abolition was that if England stopped trading in slaves and other European countries did not, they would have an unfair advantage. Even before abolition, British producers were far less efficient that their French, Spanish and Portuguese rivals.[1]

In the early session of 1807 (so that even political delaying tactics could not put it back another year), the law was finally passed abolishing the slave trade. In the House of Lords, the vote was 100 to 34 in favour; in the House of Commons it was a staggering 283 to only 16. Grenville himself described the Bill as 'the most glorious measure that had ever been adopted by any legislative body in the world'. Abolition of the slave trade passed into law on 25th March 1807.[2]

One of Bristol's MPs, Mr. Bathurst, spoke against the Bill but public opinion was now firmly in favour of abolition. Another MP, Mr. Protheroe, confirmed that, at this time, there was not a single slaver plying its trade out of Bristol.[3] Even so, her MPs (Mr. Bathurst and Colonel Bailie) still voted to maintain the trade. Mr. Protheroe was not quite accurate in his claim, as in 1807 two ships left Bristol for the coast of Africa to buy slaves: The *Swift* (380 tons; Cobb Taylor/Daniel Bryan, Master; Charles Anderson, Agent) sailed from Bristol on 4th February 1807, loaded 355 slaves and moored in Kingston, Jamaica on 11th February 1808, sold 336 slaves and arrived back at Gravesend on 29th July 1808. The other ship was the *Alert* (223 tons; William Lane, Master; Charles Anderson, Agent), the last recorded slaving ship to leave Bristol, on 20th February; she picked up 243 slaves and delivered 240 of them to Kingston, Jamaica on 16th November 1807.[4] These last few slavers could be sure of a good profit, as John Pinney wrote in 1806, in a letter, 'if those Negroes were advertised there can be no doubt of their selling at £70 sterling per head round, if not more, as the Slave trade will be completely abolished the 1st of January next.'[5]

Certainly from 1780 onwards, the number of Bristol ships involved in the slave trade had declined. For one thing, there emerged a distinct separation of the trade in slaves and that for other African produce, mainly gold, ivory and timber. The latter could prove more profitable. Between 1770 and 1776 the average rate of profit on a slave trip was 18.5%; between 1780 and 1787 this had fallen to 2.1%, and between 1788 and 1792 it reached an average of 4.2%.[6] Whether or not England was at war affected the profit, as did the rise and fall in the demand for sugar and its wholesale price, and the subsequent financial probity of the planters. What with Dolben's Law limiting the number of slaves to 1.57 for each ton of the ship, slaving was looking a less financially rewarding trade as the century reached its close. The agents for the voyages in the late part of the 18th century tended to be retired masters, rather than the old, established merchant families who had diversified into other commodities.

Still in Bristol there was a powerful reactionary feeling among the small number of ruling merchants that a rearguard action was necessary. When Baillie retired in 1812, the two MPs elected for Bristol were Mr. Richard Hart Davis, previously MP for Colchester, and Mr. Edward Protheroe. Though one was nominally a Whig and the other a Tory, they were jointly elected in the face of another Whig candidate, Sir Samuel Romily, who lost partly because of his support for the abolition of the slave trade.[7] Both Davis and Protheroe were against abolition. Supporters of Mr Protheroe produced a number of Broadsides, including one titled *Replication to the Parsons and Quakers*. They advised the Bristol public that the Quakers were supporting Romily and were making an issue of African slavery. They were accused of caring more for one suffering black man than for all their own disadvantaged white countrymen. The text included the remarkable assertion, 'Slavery, no doubt, is a bad thing.'[8]

Even after the judgements that allowed slaves to be free once they had arrived in England and this cessation of the trade out of Africa, there were still African servants in Bristol. Some were adults who had come to the city as children and who probably knew no other life; some may indeed have chosen to stay. During the Bristol Riots in 1831, the houses in Queens Square were attacked and many were burnt. The house of Mr. Claxton was threatened and a group of citizens entered the house to drive out the rioters. In the scuffles that followed, one of the rescuers, Henry Smith, a solicitor, was stabbed and Mr. Claxton's Negro butler threw one of the rioters out of an upstairs window. He had remained behind when his master had fled the city and Somerton's *Narrative* of the Riots says of him:

> 'As soon as the [rescue] party appeared, this honest fellow shouted
> 'Hurrah, massa, now for 'em', and the party, after a smart struggle, beat
> the villains out ... The black servant behaved nobly, and felled one of the
> miscreants by a blow, which caused the blood to spurt from his head
> against the walls'.[9]

In 1813 the trade with the East Indies was thrown open to competition. It was hoped that this exciting and lucrative new market would compensate for the problems with North America, the West Indies and Europe. In fact, Bristol sent out 2 ships in 1814 and the first arrival from the East Indies docked in 1818; from that time on, few ships followed this trade route from Bristol, and the anticipated wealth failed to materialise.[10]

In 1814 the Congress of Vienna was held and the British abolitionists used this meeting of European nations to raise the subject of the ending of the slave trade throughout Europe. Clarkson circulated his pamphlets to the Kings and Ministers attending (the Emperor of Russia claimed that images of the slaves in transit made him physically sick) and campaigned in France to raise abolition fervour to match that of England. He almost succeeded but the return of Napoleon put abolition once more to the rear of political consideration in Europe.[11]

Locally, the call for the emancipation of slaves carried on apace. The disapproval of the religious communities was made visible in paintings. Samuel Colman (1780-1845) was an artist who lived in Bristol from 1816-1838. He belonged to the Castle Green and Zion Independent Chapels and was an abolitionist. In his painting, *St. James's Fair* (1824), at the Bristol Museum and Art Gallery, a bookstall is shown that is kept by a Quaker couple; a customer is reading a copy of a racing guide, whilst the Quaker bookseller points to a sign reading, *In the Press: Slavery, a Poem*, which refers to a work by Hannah More. In 1820 Colman painted a *Portrait of a Negro Gentleman*; there is no reference as to who this gentleman may be, and the picture has been sold to a private collector and is not available for research. He also painted *St. John Preaching in the Wilderness*, in which a converted white solider wraps a black man in his cloak, a reference to the Biblical quotation, 'I was naked, and ye clothed me'. In the foreground is another black man, kneeling in a pose similar to that of the slave on the Anti-Slavery medallion, 'Am I not a Man and a Brother?'.

It is easier to gauge the attitudes of the pro-slavery merchants and of the abolitionists who produced such a volume of material supporting their various opinions. It is harder to judge the attitudes of the ordinary people of Bristol. However, in the early 1800s broadsides, printed sheets which sold for a few pence, were on sale to the general public. They reported items of news, put forward political, moral or religious points and generally acted as early tabloid newspapers. In Bristol Central Library is an undated *Scrapbook of Broadsides*, assembled in the early 1800s by W E Thomas which includes two papers that indicate that the subject of race could be treated with humour. The first (no 9) is titled, *A full, true and particular account of A Lady Who Longed for Charcoal, and was safely delivered this morning of a Fine Black Boy, in the neighbourhood of Guinea Street* and describes how a wife is pregnant and tells her husband that she has a longing for charcoal biscuits. When the child is born dark skinned, she says it must be the effect of all the charcoal; however, when the husband opens his wife's closet, he finds mounds of uneaten biscuits. The writer of this squib suggests a pertinent factor might be, '…visits of a black young man, a Mate of a Ship, who had brought her some sweetmeats from abroad…'

The second (No 30) is titled, *An Account of a Stone Cutter's Wife of the Hotwells who was safely delivered of Twins on Monday night last, January 7 – one a fine girl and the other A Black Boy, together with a diverting dialogue which took place between the Husband and Wife, on the appearance of the sable stranger*. The wife's explanation is that she was out walking when she suddenly met the black footman of some friends who lived in Clifton and the surprise caused her child to bear the same dark skin. Again, the sly suggestion is that the lady and the footman did rather more than bump into each other in the street. These two examples present the women as foolish and the white men as fools, but do not appear to present the black men in a negative way or suggest that they were at fault.

Wedgewood dish. This iconic image, designed by William Hackwood, for Josiah Wedgewood, showed a kneeling slave in chains with the legend, 'Am I not a Man and a Brother?'. It was extensively used and brought the abolition message to a wide public audience. (Wisbech and Fenland Museum)

In 1816 Wilberforce suggested that Parliament order a slave register to be set up in all British colonies, to ensure that no illegal slave trading was being done. The indignation of the planters and merchants was immediate at this suggestion that they might break the law! Bristol MPs presented a petition opposing the Bill, which was not enacted.[12]

Meanwhile, the East Indian merchants were lobbying as hard for an end to slavery which they claimed favoured the West Indian producers who were, in effect, being subsidised in their production costs with abnormally cheap labour. William Naish wrote *Reasons for using East India Sugar* in 1828 and suggested that the preferential treatment given the West Indian planters by the British Government encouraged absenteeism, leaving estates run by managers who wasted land and Negro lives, neither of which belonged to them.

Absenteeism was a major problem. A plantation owner like John Pinney might write from Bristol to his Manager on Nevis:

> *'Your own good sense must tell you that they [slaves] are the sinews of a plantation and must claim your particular care and attention. Humanity tempered with justice towards the former must ever be exercised, and when sick I am satisfied they will experience every kindness from you, they surely deserve it, being the very means of our support.'*

However, his manager from 1768 to 1785 was his cousin, Joseph Gill, who took to drink, paid little attention to business, failed to keep adequate records or to report to Pinney, and allowed the quality of the sugar exported to drop. John Pinney brought his cousin back to England and set him up as caretaker in one of his houses – Gill, he decided, was not suited to work in the West Indies. His next manager, William Coker, did too much, spent too much money, and would not take instruction from Pinney. He lasted until 1790, when he was replaced by yet another relative, a brother-in-law, Thomas Weekes. This young man ran mad with new ideas for 'improving' the working of the estate, which ended up reducing its profitability. In 1794 Weekes was ousted and the new manager was the ex-overseer, James Williams; he and his successor, his brother Henry, were equally unsuccessful, running into debt. The care of the slaves was very low in the list of priorities of all these men – feathering their own nests was high. Many of the managers were those who had failed in England (sometimes because of drunkenness or insanity) and who were sent to the Indies to make a fortune or at least cease to trouble their families and friends.[13]

In 1821 Wilberforce was chairman of a new group, the Society for Mitigating and Gradually Abolishing the State of Slavery, which would become known as the Anti-Slavery Society. Clarkson, co-opted on to the Committee, produced a pamphlet on the subject, *Thoughts on the Necessity for Improving the Condition of Slaves in the British Colonies, with a View to their Ultimate Emancipation, and the Practicality, Safety and Advantages of the Latter Measure.*[14] Almost immediately, due to his advancing years and ill health,

Wilberforce stood down, and Thomas Fowell Buxton took the chair. A Bristol branch of the Anti-Slavery Society was formed in October 1824; Clarkson, 62 years old and still active in the fight, addressed the inaugural meeting. On 2 February 1826 a meeting was held and the results published as *The Proceedings of the Anti-Slavery Meeting held at the Guildhall, Bristol*, printed by John Bonner, 3 Narrow Wine Street, Bristol. It was first resolved:

> 'That this Meeting laments the unhappy state of upwards of 800,000 of their fellow subjects in the colonies of Great Britain, who are in abject and degrading bondage, liable to sale and transfer, and are thus reduced to the level of brutes; a condition which this Meeting considers to be a violation of every principle of humanity and justice, contrary to the soundest maxims of national policy, and wholly repugnant to the spirit of Christianity'.[15]

Reformed characters like Mr. Lunell, an ex-slave trader, described how 'we fitted out ships for the coast, then loaded them with Negroes, took them to the Islands, where were sold for merchandise.' Mr Richard Ash answered those who claimed that the slaves were better off in their present state than if they were free, when he said : 'I will grant all the slaves are better off than the peasantry of this country, that they are better fed, better clothed and less worked – still, Sir, they are SLAVES!'.[16]

In 1827 the West India Society in Bristol sent £150 to London to support a petition to Parliament to stop Lord Bathurst from sending funds to the colonies to purchase the freedom of slaves – why should tax-payers money go to compensate kidnappers? In the following year, the Anti-Slavery Party held a public meeting in Bristol complaining about the fact that slavery was still in force, and re-stating their position that compensation should not be paid to slave owners – thieves, bullies and murderers.[17]

The Abolitionists produced literature like the heavily ironic broadside which read:

> 'Valuable Articles for the Slave Trade – To be Sold at under Prime Cost, in Consequence of the Expected Abolition – About Ten Million Dozen Negro Guns, at 24s. per Doz. About Three Tons Weight Hand and Feet Shackles and Thumb Screws, at 1 1/2d per Pound; About Ten Thousand Fine Gold-Laced Hats, at 10 1/2d each; Ten Thousand Gross Negro Knives, the whole cast Iron, at 14s per Gross; About Three Tons brilliant Diamond Necklaces, at 3s per Pound; About Ten Thousand Pieces fine Negro Linen, at 5 1/2d. Drawback, 1 1/2d per Yd. About Ten Thousand Doz. Negro Looking Glasses, at 3s per Doz. And Five Thousand Quarters Horse-Beans [the common food for slaves on the Middle Passage], at a very reduced Price – Enquire of the Slave Mongers – Specimens of the Whole (except the Thumb Screws, the Sight of which

it is thought would too deeply wound the Feelings of those not inclined to purchase) are Now exhibiting on the Exchange.'[18]

By 1830 the Bristol Anti-Slavery Society's formal membership had risen from 39 to 84. There had been four major public meetings and four petitions presented to Parliament between 1823 and 1830; and £562 had been raised, of which £300 had already gone to the main Society in London to carry on supporting the cause. However, the Bristol branch members were few in number, seen as being politically motivated, lacking in passion and zeal and faced by the ranks of city's governors, the merchants and the sitting politicians, who were virtually all pro-slavery.[19]

In 1830 another election was called; the Tories nominated the sitting MP, Mr. Davis, whilst the West Indian Whig MP, Mr. Bright, retired. The Whigs were divided on the question of slavery, and the Party put up Mr. James Evan Baillie, a West Indian merchant, as the official candidate. Charles Pinney, who seconded his nomination, reminded the voters of Bristol that more than half of the trade of the city depended on the West Indies and they depended upon slaves.[20] On one of the posters published during the election, under the heading *Baillie and Bristol Forever*, a similar message was sent:

> *'You are no doubt aware, Fellow Citizens, that Bristol owes all her prosperity, nay, I had almost said, her existence to her commerce with the West Indies. Without it she must sink to rise no more. Picture to your imagination, her now crowded streets, grass-grown and desolate – her glittering shops deserted, and the doors shut in her streets!!!'*[21]

Another prominent supporter was Captain Christopher Claxton, a Master on trading ships owned by Pinney and an ex-Lieutenant in the Royal Navy, who went on to manage and direct Baillie's campaign for election.

The more progressive elements within the Liberal Party set up a rival candidate, Mr. Edward Protheroe Jnr., who had been the MP for Evesham. Unfortunately, the result of the election was never in any real doubt; the merchants, bankers and upper classes of Bristol made no attempt to support Protheroe. Even his opening speech, during which time his father, who had represented Bristol as its MP, spoke on his behalf, was drowned out by a band hired to 'serenade' Baillie, and by the ringing of the church bells. The election was marred by mob violence, some of the worst originating from the crews of West Indian merchant ships. It was rumoured that they had been persuaded to attack Protheroe's headquarters at the Bush Inn, having been told that the abolition would throw their employers – and therefore themselves – out of work.[22] The *Bristol Mirror* reported:

> *'We believe that since the days of Brickdale, Burke, Daubeny, and Cruger, there has been nothing like it ... Bands of music everywhere parade*

the streets with banners, and immense trains of sailors and mechanics armed, shout 'Baillie for ever' and 'Protheroe for ever', as they pass the several stations they throw into the teeth of each other a brave defiance ... never within our knowledge have there ever been any thing like the immense quantities of placards – they cover every thing ...'.23

In the event, Messrs. Hart Davis and Baillie were elected – Davis with 5,012 votes and Baillie with 3,377; Protheroe polled 2,840, a reasonable result for him, under the circumstances.24 Directly after the election, the abolitionists tried to hold a public meeting to endorse a petition to Parliament for abolition; on the first occasion, the meeting ended in riot, due principally to the antics of Captain Claxton. The second meeting, despite noisy interruptions, resolved that they would appeal for abolition but Claxton and his supporters added a rider that there would have to be compensation – even they could see which way the wind was blowing and that they could no longer merely oppose abolition and emancipation.25

The following year, Mr. Protheroe, a vehement anti-slavery supporter, was challenged to a duel by Captain Claxton, who resented a letter that Mr. Protheroe had written in which he referred to a 'hired agent of the West Indian aristocracy'. The affair was settled without a shot being fired when Protheroe admitted that he had been referring to Claxton but that he did not believe him to be 'a hired agent in the common acceptation of the term'.26

1831 saw the emphasis move from slavery to parliamentary reform. Against the backdrop of the previous year, Messrs. Baillie and Protheroe were elected on a pro-reform ticket, and Davis withdrew from the poll when he realised he would lose. That same year saw the dreadful Bristol Riots, with so many people killed and so much damage done to the city, all in the name of reform. Charles Pinney wrote to Claxton that the riots had been, in part, a result of the demands for abolition:

'... the careless use of the terms Liberty and Slavery and the promulgation of ill-digested notions of the very elements of society ... engendered a spirit in Bristol.... it is worthy of note that this spirit arose in direct hostility to the leading interests in Bristol, and a notion was inculcated with great industry among the lower orders, that the great merchants, to whom they had been wont to look up with respect, were drawing their resources from human blood, and were collecting their revenues through the whip and slave driver. This feeling engendered, the names of slave and master became easily translatable...'27

In the same year the London-based West India Association formed a Bristol branch to lobby against emancipation. Over the next three years £445 was spent to send representatives to lobby Parliament; they were still active in 1842 when the emphasis had moved to the problems in finding free black or white labour to work on the plantations. The last President in Bristol was Thomas Daniel, a West India merchant who had received over £55,000 in compensation for the loss of his slaves.[28]

Elections in 1832 meant that Mr. Baillie, despite wishing to retire, was once again proposed by the Whig West Indian merchants; the Tories chose Sir Richard Vyvyan, a hard-line reactionary; the liberal Whigs put up Edward Protheroe again and a barrister, John Williams. The votes were closer than in previous years but Sir Richard Vyvyan and Mr. Baillie were elected, with 3,695 and 3,160 respectively, whilst Mr. Protheroe polled 3,028 and Mr. Williams, 2,739. There were claims of widespread and large-scale bribery, but a committee of the House of Commons ruled that the candidates had not known about it, and therefore the election results stood.[29]

One of the more ingenious methods of vote-rigging recorded in Bristol was related to the fact that the husband of a daughter of a Freeman of the city had a vote. This meant that unmarried daughters of Freemen were much valued during an election. Since the ladies might not wish to be married off just to ensure a vote was correctly cast for Whig or Tory, a marriage ceremony was performed with a reduced set of vows, concentrating on the 'till death do us part' element. The marriage was not registered, and after the election, when the Freeman's son-in-law had had his vote, the couple stood on either side of an open grave, and agreed that death had indeed parted them. The marriage was therefore ended and the lady once more free to bestow her hand. Since both political parties carried out these bogus marriages, no one was in a position to challenge them and demand that they be stopped.[30]

In 1833 Lord Grey's Ministry finally proposed a Bill for the abolition of slavery in all English colonies. In May, the outline of the plan was unveiled - that the slaves should not immediately become free, but should serve an 'apprenticeship' (carrying on working, but not being paid a proper wage). It was further stated that the owners should be recompensed for immediate losses with a loan of Government funds to the tune of £15,000,000. The planters complained for one last time (the Bristol representatives of the West Indian Association paid over £400 towards travel expenses to London for the purpose of lobbying), and the loan was changed to a gift and raised to £20,000,000.[31] Vyvyan had spoken for the anti-abolition faction, although he was only interested in getting more compensation and not in defending the slave system; Baillie never spoke at all.

The Act came into force in the colonies on 1st August 1834. The sum on offer was too small, according to the West Indian owners and too large, according to the abolitionists. Some of the payments came to Bristol-based merchants and planters. Estimates vary, but one computation would reckon that the Baillie family and companies (like Baillie & Ames) received compensation for 3,100 slaves in British Guiana, Trinidad, Grenada, St. Kitt's and St. Vincent's, to the tune of £110,000. Thomas and John Daniel received £102,000 for 3,400 slaves at Barbados, Antigua, Tobago, and British Guiana (£55,178 was for slaves on estates owned by the firm, the remainder for slaves on plantations for which the company held mortgages). The family of M.P. James Evan Bailie were granted some £62,000 for slaves in Trinidad and British Guiana. Others included:

The Pinneys	1,821 slaves	mostly Nevis	£36,396
Miles & Kington	1,457 slaves	Jamaica and Trinidad	£36,000
Charles Bean	553 slaves	British Guiana	£29,000
James Cunningham	1,056 slaves	Tobago	£21,000
Richard Bright	640 slaves	Jamaica	£12,000
The Alleyne family	717 slaves	Barbados	£17,000
Benjamin Bickley	530 slaves	Trinidad	£14,000
The Protheroe family	428 slaves	Jamaica	£8,500
The Bernard family	360 slaves	Jamaica	£6,700
James Cunningham	325 slaves	Jamaica	£6,800
Thomas Sealey	228 slaves	Barbados	£5,000

(Source: Marshall, Peter, *Bristol and the Abolition of Slavery* (1975), p.ii)

At the time of the abolition of the slave trade in 1807, the treatment of slaves in the West Indies was frequently as violent and arbitrary as ever. It occurred to some planters that better conditions for their slaves might lead to a natural increase in the population to compensate for the loss of imported slaves, and that more humane and less violent treatment might mean that slaves lived and worked longer. General appreciation for human rights, however, does not seem to have been considered. The Parliamentary Committee of 1789 had received a report from their clerk, John Reeves, on the state of the laws relating to slaves in the West Indies. These included such crimes as selling foodstuffs without permission of their owner, leaving their plantation without written authorisation (with times and dates), possession of any weapon, striking or 'offering insolence' to a white person, practising 'witchcraft' and the usual crimes of theft, assault and murder. The punishments ranged from whipping to hard labour, loss of a limb and execution.[32]

Notes

1   Gifford, Zerbanoo, *Thomas Clarkson and the Campaign Against Slavery* (1996), p.44-5
2   Gifford, Zerbanoo, op cit, p.46-7
3   Latimer, John, *The Annals of Bristol in the Nineteenth Century* (1887), p.29
4   Richardson, David, (ed), *Bristol, Africa and the 18th Century Slave Trade to America: The Final Years 1770-1807*, Vol.4 (1991), p.266
5   MacInnes, C.M., Bristol: A Gateway of Empire (1968), p.343
6   Richardson, David, (ed), op cit, p.xxix
7   Latimer, John, *The Annals of Bristol in the Nineteenth Century* (1887), p.51
8   Thomas, WE, *Scrapbook of Broadsides, 1824*
9   Marshall, Peter, op cit, p.23
10   Latimer, John, op cit, p.50
11   Gifford, Zerbanoo, op cit, p.50-1
12   MacInnes, C.M., *Bristol: A Gateway of Empire* (1968), p.344-5
13   Pares, Richard, *A West-Indian Fortune* (1968), p.143-7
14   Gifford, Zerbanoo, op cit, p.53
15   The Proceedings of the Anti-Slavery Meeting held at the Guildhall, Bristol (1826)
16   The Proceedings of the Anti-Slavery Meeting held at the Guildhall, Bristol (1826)
17   MacInnes, C.M. op cit, p.350-2
18   City of Bristol Industrial Museum, Reg. No. 310
19   Marshall, Peter, op cit, p.4
20   Latimer, John, op cit, p.137
21   Marshall, Peter, op cit, p.2
22   ibid p.5-9
23   ibid p.11
24   Latimer, John, op cit, p.138
25   Marshall, Peter, op cit, p.18-9
26   Latimer, John, op cit, p.145-6
27   Marshall, Peter, op cit, p.24
28   Little, Bryan, The City and County of Bristol (1967), p.259
29   Latimer, John, op cit, p.185-6
30   ibid p.411
31   ibid p.188
32   Craton, Michael, Walvin, James, & Wright, David, *Slavery, Abolition and Emancipation* (1976), p.181-90

FIFTEEN

After 1807 the cry for freedom in the West Indies intensified. In 1813 a branch of the Church of England Missionary Society for Africa and the East was set up in Bristol. Despite fervent opposition from the planters and residents, preachers of many different religious bodies tried to preach Christianity to the slaves, the foremost being the Methodists, Moravians and Baptists. The West Indian slave owners were against this teaching, not because they were against their slaves being ostensibly part of the approved church, but because, as a speaker at an ecumenical meeting at the Bristol Guildhall on 2nd February 1826 showed:

> 'It is a dangerous thing to teach slaves Christianity; you cannot teach Christianity without the Bible; you cannot withhold the Bible from slaves if you mean to teach them Christianity ... How can slaves be taught the grand maxim of elementary morality, "As you would that men should do to you, do you also unto them"? Can they read texts calling men to liberty, announcing deliverance to the captive, binding up the broken hearted?'.[1]

The governor of Demerara provided a perfect instance of the colonial attitude to missionaries. After a slave revolt, he passed a series of laws – that religious services could only be held between sunrise and sunset, when slaves would be at work; anyone preaching had to have an expensive licence; any slave found preaching without his owner's consent would be flogged. In 1823 a dissenting missionary, John Smith, was charged with fomenting rebellion and, with no evidence presented, he was sentenced to death. He died in prison, awaiting his reprieve from England.[2]

The West Indian colonial governors did very little to improve the lot of the slaves or to regulate their treatment. They seemed not to recognise that the end of the slave trade would inexorably be followed by emancipation; there was always the feeling that the British Government would support them, and fail to enact legislation against their interests, as it had always done. They had the right of property and this right would always be protected. Slaves were still beaten so badly that they could not work; families were still split up so that their grief hampered their labour. Edward Long, describing his own Jamaican estate in 1788, recorded that in 1761 the total slave population of Jamaica was 146,805. During the following 7 years, 46,917 slaves were imported, but the population in 1768 only totalled 166,904 – during that time, 26,818 slaves had been freed, left the Island, run away, disappeared or died.[3]

During the American War of Independence and after, the West Indian Islands suffered consistently from the withdrawal of their mutual commerce. In April 1822 the West Indian merchants of Bristol sent a petition to Parliament asking for restrictions on their trade with America to be lifted. They complained that they were obliged to send most of their rum and molasses to England so that there was a glut and prices fell, and that imports of sugar from the East meant that the planters made small profits. After all, the East Indian merchants only bought the sugar; they did not have the expense of growing it. Once again, the mercantile interest was successful, and a Bill was passed opening free trade between America and the West Indies.[4]

The East Indian merchants, however, struck back by petitioning in their own right for a law to do away with the unacceptably heavy duties on sugar from the East, as opposed to the West. Bristol merchants opposed this Bill, reiterating their belief that, given the recent low prices of sugar, further competition would mean ruin to the West Indian planters and consequently to Bristol as a whole. In 1826, despite pleas from Bristol and elsewhere, Parliament allowed the same duty on sugar from Mauritius as from the West Indies and two years later, added sugar from Bombay to that price level.[5]

By 1823 William Wilberforce had retired from his position as the vocal figurehead of the abolition and emancipation movement, to be replaced by Thomas Fowell Buxton. His main problem now seemed to be the level of compensation that West Indian slave owners would ask for. The idea that Negroes were happy in their lot and better off than other labourers and that the West Indian economy would collapse without them, were now a minority view of a few die-hards. Lord Bathurst was still trying to persuade the West Indian authorities to improve the conditions of the slaves, but without success. He wanted voluntary agreement that all slaves should have access to religious instruction, marriage should be encouraged and respected and that families should no longer be split up. He also suggested that punishments should be radically reduced and recorded in an estate ledger, that slaves should be allowed legal possessions (including money) without fear of their owner confiscating them and that slaves who were able, should not be hindered in buying their own freedom. The planters, fighting their rearguard action, resolutely refused to enact any of his suggestions.[6]

In the same year, James George, the Mayor of Bristol, put his name to a petition to Parliament that asked that the question of colonial abolition should be explored. The document read:

> 'Your Petitioners having considered the inconsistency of the system of Colonial Slavery with the Christian Religion as well as the danger to which the system exposed the White Inhabitants of the Colonies and the Property of the Planters generally ... require that means should be taken, without delay, gradually, cautiously and with just regard to the Rights and Property of the Colonists, as well as to the claims for Compensation ... to remove from our County that heavy responsibility, which the sanction given by the Government and the People to the System of Slavery in the Colonies, has brought upon this enlightened Nation, and to relieve a vast multitude of our suffering fellow-creatures from a lamentable state of degradation and oppression'.[7]

A group of West Indian interested parties sent a counter-petition saying that the first one did not represent the opinion of all Bristolians.

The question of compensation was not easily resolved. Some abolitionists stated that the keepers of slaves did not deserve any compensation at all, since the slaves were kidnapped prisoners in the first place – should you compensate a thief who is forced to give back his stolen booty? One writer to the letters page of *Felix Farley's Bristol Journal* suggested that the various anti-slavery groups should pool their resources and buy all the slaves at a reasonable valuation. They should then set a small price on each slave, and then when the slave had earned this small sum, they could 'buy' their freedom from their 'owners'. This would mean that the government would not have to pay compensation, and at the same time the planters would not be out of pocket.[8]

The Anti-Slavery Society was against compensation, alleging that not only had the planters bought men and women as slaves, but had abused, beaten, mutilated and murdered them as well. The two sides of the debate were now crystallising around those who opposed compensation and those who supported some form of it. In the years immediately preceding colonial abolition, there were a series of incidents in the colonies, involving slaves who had heard rumours of emancipation and tried to seize their freedom as a consequence. In 1815 and again in 1823 and 1824, there were unsuccessful slave revolts in Jamaica (in 1815 one of the ring-leaders was transported to Australia); in 1816 there was one in Barbados, in 1823 in British Guiana and in 1831, in Antigua.[9]

In 1831 in Jamaica, a revolt headed by Sam Sharpe involved 20,000 slaves refusing to work under conditions of slavery after 27th December. They had heard that slavery had been abolished in England, and knew that the French slaves on Haiti had fought for and won their independence. It took the Governor and troops two months to subdue the rebellion; 272 rebels were executed, including one woman, 21 were transported and many more were imprisoned, flogged and sentenced to hard labour. Sharpe spoke for the rebels and for many of the slaves when he told the Rev. Bleby, who visited him in prison before his execution, 'I would rather die upon yonder gallows than live in slavery'. There had been over £1,000,000-worth of damage done and the cost of the armed forces action was £162,000. Missionaries were blamed; their chapels were razed, and they were arrested, tried and deported, with no evidence presented. They were seen as a bad influence, partly because they taught slaves to read, so that they could see in the British papers how the situation on abolition and emancipation was going.[10] American supporters of slavery had actually suggested that any public discussion of the rights and wrongs of slavery should be banned as it would lead to slaves learning about their situation. This in turn would make them become discontented and rebellious. This would make owners act even more cruelly in order to maintain discipline. Thus, they claimed, discussion of the issue only made the lot of the slaves worse.[11]

The planters used these events to show that the slaves were not ready for freedom. The British government continued to send out protests and suggestions for reform. These included the 'radical' suggestions that women should no longer be flogged, that field workers should not be beaten as they laboured, that families should not be split up and sold separately, that slaves should have free access to Christian worship. These suggestions usually caused the colonial owners to complain even more loudly about the need for gradual emancipation and the slaves' unfitness to run their own affairs. In fact, the persistence of the revolts may have persuaded the slave owners that they would have to accept some form of emancipation, and that sooner rather than later.

In the end, in 1833, the Government came down on the side of emancipation with compensation. As of 1st August 1834, children aged six or less were to be deemed to be free immediately. Those who were domestic servants (skilled) would serve an 'apprenticeship' of four years, and field workers (unskilled) would serve six years. They would stay on the plantation to which they had formerly belonged, and be paid only for any time they worked over a standard 40 hours which they had to give for free to their 'employer'.[12] Twenty million pounds was made available for compensation to the slave owners – nothing was set aside to give to the slaves.[13]

In 1835, election to the Jamaican Assembly was opened to those of mixed race; one of the first elected was Edward Jordan, a free black who had been imprisoned for publishing a newspaper, *The Watchman*, which advocated emancipation by force, if necessary.[14] He and others fought against the apprenticeship system, which was a disgrace. The slaves were still bound to serve their ex-owners without payment. They were denied the chance to earn money to buy land (what money they did make went to pay exorbitant rents for their home and patch of land) and they had no guarantee that wages due to them would be paid. They could be arrested on frivolous charges and, thanks to dissolute magistrates, still savagely punished – for example, anyone not working for a recognised employer was a vagrant, subject to arrest and flogging. The apprentice system was abolished in Jamaica in 1838[15] – Antigua and Bermuda had decided to free all their slaves immediately on 1st August 1834.[16]

It was not the immediate total disaster predicted by the West Indian interest groups. Lord Sligo, the Governor of Jamaica, wrote:

> 'The first prophecy was blood and destruction on the 1st of August; in this they were wrong. The second, that this scene would take place at Christmas; in this they were wrong. The third, that the apprentices would not work for wages; in this they were wrong, as I know of no instance in which the usual wages were offered and were refused. The fourth was that the crop would not be taken off; in this they were wrong, as it has in many cases been taken off much earlier than usual, and if protracted in others, it has been as much from the weather and the refusal to give wages in many instances, as from any other cause...'[17]

However, there were problems that led to a final reduction of planting. Even in 1842, complaints were made to the British Government that the colonists were finding it difficult to get free black or white workers to replace the slaves they had lost. The cost of sugar rose accordingly as costs of production rose and the removal of import duties on sugar from other parts of the world also caused financial hardship to the Caribbean planters. In 1830 some 63% of Bristol's trade was with the West Indies; by 1840 this was down to 40% and by 1871 it was further reduced to 29%.[18] The sugar industry in Bristol survived the West Indian troubles by importing sugar from alternative sources and modernising production as Britain entered the Industrial Revolution. The new breed of industrialists wanted cheap sugar for their low-waged workers, and they had no desire to support the West Indian planters to their own detriment.

Not all plantation owners were uncaring and not all slaves were treated with vile cruelty. In January 1815 Mr. Samuel Gist, a Virginia planter, died and left a number of bequests. He had been educated at Queen Elizabeth Hospital, Bristol, and left £10,000 to form a trust that would be used to financially support thee poor men and three women, and to educate three boys at Queen Elizabeth Hospital and three girls at the Red Maids' School. He also willed their freedom to his 300 slaves in Virginia and set up a trust for them to provide education, including religious instruction, for them and their descendants as well as providing support, food and clothes for any who should fall on hard times.[19]

John Pinney, who lived at the Georgian House in Great George Street, was a West Indian merchant and planter who returned to Bristol in 1783 to retire. In July 1772 he and his wife had left Nevis to go on their honeymoon attended by her maid Nancy Jones and his servant Pero, both Africans. In May 1798, in Bristol, Pinney wrote to a friend in London:

> 'Every branch of my family save my son Charles who has a Cold are perfectly well – I must also except my servant Pero who is very ill and now at Ashton for change of Air. I much doubt his recovery – one or other of us visit him three or four times a week. He has waited on my Person upwards of thirty two years, and I cannot help feeling much for him: notwithstanding he has not lately conducted himself as well as I could have wished.'

On November 12, Pinney wrote to a friend on Nevis:

> 'Pero, I am sorry to inform you, died a few months ago, after being almost useless to me for a considerable time before his death, caused by Drunkenness and Dissipation – Almost since we left Nevis in 1794 – his conduct has been very reprehensible – insomuch, that his Mistress and every branch of my Family have urged me to Discharge him and to send

*him back to Nevis with an Annual allowance: provided his behaviour there
should have deserved it.* [20]

Pero had reason for the depression that led to his drinking. On the family's last visit
to the West Indies he had formed an attachment with a young lady and had been
given the choice of staying with her as a slave in the harsh conditions that prevailed,
or returning to Bristol. Add the fact that she may have had his child and Pero's
depression seems far more understandable.

Another much loved servant was Samuel Thompson, who died in 1806. His
tombstone reads:

> *'In memory of Samuel Thompson, late servant to William Thompson
> of Jamaica Esqr., who was unfortunately drowned in the Avon on 16th
> August 1806 aged 20 years. This stone is laid as a testimony of the Regard
> his Master bears him, memory for his services which since the early Age of
> 7 years he has discharged faithfully and with integrity. He died lamented
> by his Master and all who knew him'.*

The tragic story of Samuel's death was published in *Felix Farley's Bristol Journal* for
23rd August, which described how he had been swimming in the river opposite St.
Vincent's Rocks, was seized with cramp and drowned; 'His body was not found until
Sunday morning'. [21]

Samuel Thompson, like so many others, had come to England with his
owner/master from the West Indies. Bristol churches record several Afro-Caribbeans,
like Samuel Davy, 'a black of Black River, Jamaica. a good 25 years', baptised at St.
Paul's in October 1800, and Elizabeth Guy, baptised at St. Nicholas, December 1803,
'an adult Negro of the island of Nevis, about 51 years old'. [22] An explanation for the
presence of Africans in Bristol at this time is given in the autobiography of the slave
known as Mary Prince, who published her life story in 1831. [23] She was born into
slavery in Bermuda and ended up working for a family, the Jameses, in Antigua, who
treated her with vicious cruelty. The couple came to England to see to the education
of their children, bringing Mary with them as a maid of all works and attendant for
the girls. Once in England, they threatened to turn her out of the house when she
complained about the hard work they expected her to do as a laundress, even though
she was crippled with rheumatism. Fortunately, Mary was a devout Moravian and
was able to receive guidance and support from her church in London who helped her
to break away and make a life for herself. She remarked that others of her
countrymen, finding themselves in a strange land whose language they spoke
imperfectly, with no money and no contacts, often remained in virtual slavery as the
alternative was starvation in the streets of some English town. It may be that some ex-
slaves stayed with fair and reasonable employers of their own will, but many were
terrorised into servitude and feared freedom as much as slavery.

The wealth generated from the slave trade financed new houses, streets and crescents in the fashionable suburbs, particularly Clifton. 'From Mrs Lee's Window at Number 11 Lower Crescent, Clifton.' Lower Crescent is now known at Cornwallis Crescent. In the distance is the tower in the grounds of Goldney House. R.S. Sanders 1850 (Bristol's Museums, Galleries & Archives)

The fate of the Africans who remained in Bristol can often only be guessed at. A group of newspaper cuttings[24] dating from the first quarter of the 19th century show how at least one element of the black population made a living performing display bouts of bare-knuckle boxing:

> *'The match between Carter and Robin the Black was decided on Thursday last, on Moulsey-hurst, in the presence of at least 20,000 spectators ... The Black gave in in Round 12 ... "I'll fight no more" ... The black's head was miserably disfigured.'*

> *'A day's play took place on Tuesday at Coombe Warren, between no less than 6 candidates for prizes. The chief attraction, however, was a novel exhibition between Joseph Stevenson, as so termed, and Sam. Robinson, both blacks, for 40 guineas'; Robinson won in the 40th round.*

There are a few examples of slaves who achieved freedom and then left their mark on British society. Olaudah Equiano and Ignatius Sancho both wrote books of great importance to the abolition cause. *The Eighth Report of the Directors of the African Institution*, London, 1814, reported a further success story. James Martin had been bought as a slave in the West Indies but had ended up in Bristol, attained his freedom and made enough money to leave a legacy to the African Association for Missionary Work in Africa.[25]

Not all slaves, of course, were respected family servants. Many, when they reached England, were unwanted once they had achieved their freedom, had to be paid and treated as freemen and women. Certainly in London, and possibly, to a lesser extent, in Bristol, abandoned slaves became part of the statistics of the poor and destitute. In 1790 an attempt was made to provide a home for emancipated slaves and to found a trading settlement for fair trade with Africa. Land in Sierra Leone was given to this project and a joint stock company was formed that would have special privileges in matters of trade between England and Africa. Not unsurprisingly, groups like the Bristol Merchant Venturers were radically opposed to such a company, as it would severely disadvantage them in profitable trade. Bristol ships were reputed to be the most frequent visitors to Brent (also known as Bence or Bunce) Island on the Sherbro River in Sierra Leone, supplying 'necessaries' like strong beer, wine and cyder.[26] Sierra Leone, with its good year-round anchorage, had always been a free port, even to the extent of being free to French traders under the terms of the Treaty of Versailles in 1783. The Merchant Venturers authorised the spending of funds on opposition in Parliament. In the event, the Sierra Leone Company was given its charter; interestingly enough, several prominent abolitionists were amongst its first directors.[27]

It has been estimated that there were between 15,000 and 20,000 slaves in England when the slave trade was abolished and emancipation was imminent. The slaves were

Samuel Colman (1780-1845) was an artist and abolitionist who lived in Bristol from 1816-1838. In his painting, St. James's Fair (1824), at the Bristol Museum and Art Gallery, a bookstall is shown that is kept by a Quaker couple. Hanging from the awning of the stall is a sign: 'In the Press: slavery, a Poem' which refers to a work by Hannah More. Detail of St James Fair. (Bristol's Museums, Galleries & Archives).

treated in one of three ways – they were sent to the West Indies (sometimes forcibly, as has been noted), they were 'absorbed' into the community (for example, pensioned off, kept on as paid servants, or thrown out on to the streets) or they were sent or persuaded to go to Africa, particularly to Sierra Leone.[28]

The settlement of Freetown, Sierra Leone, had been the brainchild of Granville Sharpe who, in 1787, had founded what he called the Province of Freedom as a home for freed slaves who wished to return to Africa, but had nowhere to go back to. The town grew up on St. George's Bay, a large, natural harbour that gave it strong trading advantages. After initial setbacks, including attacks by a local chieftain and by slave traders, Sharpe arranged for British merchants to provide supplies to the colonists in return for trade agreements. Education and training also formed a part of the deal. In 1789 a group of 50 boys and 25 girls were sent to England for education from Sierra Leone; some of them came to Bristol, as well as going to London, Liverpool and Lancaster.[29]

To further the trade, the settlers were formed into the Sierra Leone Company, which received its charter from the British Government in 1791. Alexander Falconbridge became a commercial agent in Sierra Leone in that year. Three years earlier he had been a witness before Parliament, reporting on his time as a ship's surgeon on slaver's voyages that so disgusted him that he became a witness for the anti-slavery lobby. His time with the Sierra Leone company, however, was brief. He had a drink problem, was dismissed almost immediately and died not long after from a combination of an unhealthy climate and alcoholic abuse.[30]

The Sierra Leone Company issued shares and its shareholders and its early directors included Sharpe and Clarkson, who had always favoured honest trade with Africa as a way forward. Other shareholders included abolitionists, merchants and bankers who sympathised with the aims of Sharpe and Clarkson – as well as some MPs with guilty consciences about voting against abolition, it was rumoured.[31]

The ex-slaves came from many places. In 1815 a wealthy American ex-slave, Paul Cuffee, paid for 38 freed slaves to be relocated to Sierra Leone. Not content with this, he also put his own money into an export business, sending African goods to America, the West Indies and Europe.[32] In the early years, Clarkson's brother, John, brought a group of more than a thousand from Canada; many of them had fought for the British army in the American War of Independence and had ended up in Nova Scotia when they were forced to flee the newly independent country. John Clarkson became a popular governor of Sierra Leone.[33]

In 1807, with abolition of the slave trade, the Sierra Leone Company too was abolished and Sierra Leone became a full British colony. In 1814 Clarkson founded a new group, the 'Society for Encouraging the Black Settlers at Sierra Leone, and the Natives of Africa generally, in the Cultivation of their Soil, by the Sale of their Produce'. This made Sierra Leone one of the first areas to trade with Britain on fair terms.

With ex-slaves returning in larger numbers, by 1850 there were more than 50,000 living in Sierra Leone. As Britain's first African colony, the country achieved independence in 1961.[34]

CONCLUSION

Derek Robinson put the number of slaves transported from Africa to the Americas between 1698 (the official opening of the trade to Bristol) and 1807 (abolition of the slave trade) as 7-10 million. He estimated that 74,000 were transported in 1788 alone.[35] James Walvin recorded that the figure is open to wide interpretation, being estimated at anything from 10 to 25 million.[36] David Richardson suggested from the records available that between 1698 and 1807, Bristol was the recorded point of origin of about 2,000 ships engaged in the slave trade. Calculating that an average of 250 slaves a voyage reached the port of destination, that meant that Bristol ships alone transported in excess of 500,000 slaves from Africa to America and the West Indies. There are no precise figures for the number of captives who died on the march to the coast; how many died waiting for a ship; how many died during loading; how many died on the crossing; how many died before they could be unloaded; how many died before they could be set to work. There are no precise numbers for the Africans labouring in the Americas and the Caribbean. The actual volume of this trade will never be fully known; only the echoes of the Transatlantic Slave Trade remain today.

Notes

1   Ballard, Martin, *Bristol Sea-Port City* (1966), p.90-1
2   Sherwood, Marika, *Black Peoples in the Americas* (1992), p.87
3   Craton, Michael, Walvin, James, Wright, David, *Slavery, Abolition and Emancipation* (1976), p.106
4   Latimer, John, *The Annals of Bristol in the Nineteenth Century* (1887), p96-7
5   Latimer, John, op cit, p106-7
6   Sherwood, Marika, op cit, p.91
7   MacInnes, C.M. *Bristol: A Gateway to Empire* (1968), p.347-8
8   MacInnes, C.M., op cit (1968), p.349
9   Sherwood, Marika, op cit (1992), p.87
10   ibid p.88-9
11   McColley, Robert, *Slavery and Jeffersonian Virginia* (1964), p.118-9
12   Craton, Michael, Walvin, James & Wright, David, op cit, p.325-6
13   Latimer, John, op cit, p.188
14   Sherwood, Marika, op cit, p.73, 88
15   ibid p.88
16   Williams, Eric, Capitalism and Slavery (1964), p.191
17   Craton, Michael, Walvin, James, Wright, David, op cit, p.330
18   MacInnes, C.M. *Bristol: A Gateway of Empire* (1968), p.370-1
19   Latimer, John, op cit, p.62
20   Pinney Letter Books, University of Bristol Library
21   Mary V Campbell, *Memorials of the Church and Churchyard of St Andrews, Clifton* (1987), No. 3667
22   Lindegaard, DP, *Bristol Roots: Black Bristolians in the 17th, 18th and 19th Centuries* (1990), p.18, 22
23   Moira Ferguson (ed), *The History of Mary Prince, A West Indian Slave, Related by Herself*, 1987
24   Untitled album, Bristol Central Reference Library
25   Walvin, James, *Black and White, The Negro and English Society 1555-1945* (1973), p.64
26   Craton, Michael, Walvin, James & Wright, op cit, p.24
27   MacInnes, C.M. op cit, p.339-40
28   Thomas, Hugh, Observer Colour Supplement, 17 October 1965.
29   Walvin, James, *Black and White, The Negro and English Society 1555-1945* (1973), p.51
30   Marshall, Peter, *'The Anti-Slave Trade Movement in Bristol'*, McGrath, Patrick (ed.), *Bristol in the Eighteenth Century* (1972), p.204
31   Gifford, Zerbanoo, op cit, p.35
32   Sherwood, Marika, op cit, p.74
33   Gifford, Zerbanoo, op cit.35
34   ibid p.36
35   Robinson, Derek, *A Shocking History of Bristol* (1973), p.57
36   Walvin, James, *Slavery and the Slave Trade* (1983), p.40

INDEX